HEDGING FOREIGN EXCHANGE

HEDGING FOREIGN EXCHANGE

CONVERTING RISK TO PROFIT

Eric T. Jones

Donald L. Jones

JOHN WILEY & SONS

New York • Chichester • Brisbane • Toronto • Singapore

Library of Congress Cataloging in Publication Data:

Jones, Eric T. (Eric Thomas)
  Hedging foreign exchange.

  Bibliography: p.
  1. Forward exchange. 2. Foreign exchange.
3. Hedging (Finance) 4. Risk. I. Jones, Donald L.
II. Title.
HG3853.J66 1987   332.4′5   86-26639
ISBN 0-471-84986-3

Printed in the United States of America

10 9 8 7 6 5 4 3 2 1

KP

To our mothers
Always supportive.

Preface

The inability of the central banks of the world to stabilize currency exchange rates has been readily apparent. Over the past several years the quarterly volatility of exchange rates has been as high as 25 percent of the total value of a currency. At times exchange rate volatility is the largest risk faced by the businessperson. The accounting profession has recognized this large and growing problem with the creation of FAS-8 and, later, FAS-52. However, recognizing and accounting for losses and/or gains is hardly the same as avoiding the risk altogether. One approach to risk avoidance is called hedging and it is the subject of this book.

The number and variety of hedging techniques have increased with the volatility of the currency marketplace. The selection is already large and growing. Many techniques are considered trade secrets. Those that are published are often highly convoluted. For the beginner, the fundamentals must be mastered before applications can be understood. This book starts with first principles. The interaction between the company, the market, and taxation is carefully traced. The why, what, where, and when of currency hedging are developed. Only then are actual techniques explored and evaluated. The authors will consider the book a success if its use helps a wide class of readers to actually evaluate their foreign exchange risk and to formulate and execute their own hedging strategies.

This book is designed to be a *how to* or *where to go to find out how to* for both the large multinational and the relatively small hedger. In addition, its broad scope and use of real time series data to support and explain the theory make this book useful both as a college sourcebook and a guide for those developing hedging or trading programs. The material is sectioned into two basic parts: (1) methods for recognizing and handling risk within the confines of the operation, and (2) technical hedging techniques for exposures of a specific size and duration. Part 1 introduces the fundamentals of foreign exchange risk measurement and management. It is recognized that developing a quality risk management program requires a clear understanding of virtually every area of financial management. The early chapters of Part 1 strive to reduce these seemingly complex areas to concepts understandable by all. Exposure and exposure measurement are detailed first with exposure management following. Dozens of risk management techniques, accessible both from within and outside the organization, are introduced and explained. The wide variance in needs by each particular company precludes a case by case study. Close attention is paid to the effects of taxation, accounting standards, and country currency regulations. The general principles covered should be able to provide guidance for any individual situation.

Part 2 breaks new ground in the technical analysis of hedging. It presumes a known exposure as well as a commitment to hedge. This section begins by defining three types of technical hedge (hedge and hold, modified hedge and hold, and selective hedge). It then discusses the drawbacks of fundamental economic analysis as a basis for hedge selection. Next, it defines technical analysis and the difference between technical analysis and chart analysis. The theoretical basis for technical analysis is developed and the random walk theory is shown to not apply to futures markets and, by extension, to forwards or options. A discussion of two standard trading models that have been profitable on the British pound since 1976 follows. It is noted that trading is not hedging, but that trading models can provide the requisite timing for the initiation of a hedge. Then a case study of eight years of hedging the British pound with the selective hedge demonstrates the profitability of that type of hedge for both the long and short hedgers. Next, the findings of Part 2 are overlaid on Part 1, as selectively timing the hedge is shown to apply equally well to traditional, internal methods. Lastly, advice is given on the makeup of a hedging group within the operations of the hedger.

The bulk of the detailed analyses involves futures despite the fact that more than 90 percent of today's external foreign exchange activity is accomplished in the interbank market. There are good reasons for this decision. First and foremost is the existence of a daily auction market posted in futures; that is not the case for forwards or the cash market. Options on the Philadelphia Exchange and on the International Monetary Market trade throughout the day, providing continuous price discovery. So it is possible to scope the futures market (high, low, range, volatility, etc.). For the technician, this is a significant plus in evaluating market descriptors. A most important point is that even though the analyses are done on futures, one does not have to hedge there. The timing derived from the models is just as easily applied to forwards, options, or internal methods.

The authors intend this book to be an aid to all levels of exposure managment as well as an initiation into the field of technical analysis. Its aim is to be a working manual in this most important field.

Eric Jones
Donald Jones

Chicago, IL
March 1987

Contents

PART 2   CONVERTING RISK TO PROFIT

Part 1

Hedging Foreign Exchange

INTRODUCTION

Since late 1971, central bankers have permitted their currencies to float. And floated they have, at times by as much as 25 percent of their total value in three months' time. Faced with the prospect of potential losses created by fluctuations of this magnitude, companies can no longer afford to buy, sell, or operate abroad unprotected. For today's international financial managers, protection is the name of the game and safe hedging is the bottom line.

Operating internationally differs in many respects from operating just within one's own country. There are different cultures, economies, governments, laws, and monies. But time's impact on currency values is the added dimension that clearly separates trading at home from trading abroad. Time creates uncertainty. Time lapses between the date of sale and the date of payment, between dividends declared and dividends paid, and so forth, provide the opportunity for currencies to move. The price of money fluctuates for good economic reasons that will not go away. Causes are changes in the productivity of the work force, the spending of politicians, relative trade advantages, and things of this sort. These factors are continually changing, sometimes very rapidly. Foreign exchange transactions conducted in this environment are said to be *exposed*. In the face of today's volatile markets, hedging foreign currency exposure is a recognized necessity.

Hedging takes many forms. Many companies without foreign subsidiaries (e.g., import/export firms) simply make it their policy to invoice only in their own currency. This way, the contracted price is exactly what is received or paid, regardless of what happens in the currency markets (see Chapter 9). Companies that operate in many countries usually employ a variety of more sophisticated techniques to protect their exposures. Regardless, a well-placed hedge is only as sound as the definition of the exposure it is designed to cover. The exposure must first be recognized and then measured correctly. This groundwork, exposure recognition and measurement, is fundamental to every hedging program.

The chapters within Part 1 introduce the concept and handling of currency risk in simple, practical terms. Chapter 1 examines the reasons why corporations should hedge their foreign currency exposures. A glance at many corporate financial statements suggests that this need has already been established. Chapter 2 discusses the different types of exposure that may confront the hedger, where exposure occurs, and how to measure it. Once the exposure is known, protecting or *neutralizing* it becomes the next matter of business. This is covered in Chapter 3 in considerable detail. Topics range from transfer pricing to foreign currency options. A summary of important tax considerations and a mention of the types of currency controls and regulations placed by countries are also presented. Part 1 closes with Chapter 6, a discussion of what is being done by a number of firms today. Chapter 6 presents and analyzes the results of a limited 1984 hedging survey of U.S. corporations, both large and small. Part 2 augments Part 1 by introducing technical market analysis as a unique and valuable tool for managing foreign currency exposure, a tool offering both protection and the potential for profit.

1
Historical Background

In August 1971, President Nixon announced that the U.S. dollar would no longer be convertible into gold. This event transformed a fixed, relatively predictable foreign exchange market into a market of floating and highly irregular rates. Prior to Nixon's announcement central bankers managed exchange rates within the confines of Bretton Woods. The Bretton Woods agreement of 1944 established the International Monetary Fund and the agreement that all member countries would value their currencies at either a given amount of gold or a specified number of U.S. dollars ($35/ounce). For 20 years thereafter, the world was confident that U.S. gold reserves were sufficient to fulfill the United States' dollar/gold exchange guarantee. Currency rates generally hovered within their established ranges. Fluctuation rarely exceeded 1 to 2 percent. Only the players with extremely large positions saw a benefit to hedging. Then came the wave of increasing U.S. expenditures, led by the Vietnam War and fed by the expansionary fiscal policies that are so familiar today. By 1971 the number of dollars in circulation exceeded the value of U.S. gold reserves. World confidence in the dollar diminished rapidly, European central banks allowed their currencies to float and the dollar began to depreciate against most currencies. Since 1973, exchange rates have continued to float. With but a few exceptions, the float has been surprisingly free.

Exchange rates are influenced by a great number of underlying economic and political factors. Some are real economic conditions such as a country's economic prosperity, comparative advantage, and so forth. Others are contrived, as in the intervention of central banks into the foreign exchange markets to maintain or influence desirable exchange rate levels. But regardless of how or why currencies move, the fact that they do and will continue to move poses a serious business risk to the firm. Businesses are uncomfortable with this risk, but few hedge. The lack of hedging probably stems from the newness of the risk and the lack of well-known techniques for handling it.

WHAT IS A HEDGE?

The fact that there are countless ways to hedge has already been noted. What has not yet been discussed is the hedge itself. Most currency hedges consist of offsetting positions in the same currency. These appear in many different forms, but all are intended to accomplish the same task. For starters, think of a hedge as an insurance policy, not unlike the policy you take out on your home, your car, or yourself. If you lose a leg your insurance company gives you, say, $50,000 for the loss. You are compensated more if you have the misfortune to lose both legs. Similarly, a currency hedge is designed to compensate for losses created by unforeseen bad exchange rate luck. If exchange rates suddenly move to your disadvantage and foreign revenues turn out not to be what were planned, a properly managed hedge can make up the difference. In a sense, proper hedge management means that your business legs are a lot less likely to be cut out from under you.

Let us assume that a U.S. firm owns a substantial portion of stock in a West German company. The value of the stock and its earnings fluctuate with the performance of the company. But what happens if the value of the deutsche mark increases relative to the dollar? In dollar terms, the value of the U.S. company's West German holdings falls. What can the U.S. firm do to combat the potential loss? The answer is quite simple. Holding the West German stock is akin to lending the West German company deutsche marks. So it makes sense that borrowing an equal amount of deutsche marks would create the offsetting position that the firm is looking for. As the deutsche mark rises the dollar value of the borrowing falls. Thus fewer dollars are needed to pay both the interest and the principal. In the end, losses on the West German investment are made up by gains on the borrowing. There are many other ways to "take the other side." Many businesses forgo the complications often accompanied by foreign borrowing (unless they have a specific use for it) and simply enter into a bank forward contract. Futures or options might do the job too (Chapter 3 describes these methods, and others as well).

Hedging differs from company to company. Smaller businesses with only a few foreign transactions each year can choose to hedge each transaction, or exposure, as the need arises. On the contrary, multinationals face many exposure problems every day. They surface in all areas, from division to division, subsidiary to subsidiary, and company to company. How to manage multiple exposures ultimately depends on the organization's overall structure and objectives. Some companies centralize their hedging functions, with the parent company directing all hedging decisions from headquarters. Others are decentralized with each unit (parent and subsidiary) responsible for its own hedging decisions. While both approaches effectively get the same job done, each has advantages over the other. The centralized approach generally results in more efficient hedge management and, therefore, lower hedge costs. The drawback to this approach is the fact that subsidiaries tend to have little control over their own foreign exchange risk. A global protection strategy of this sort implies that each subsidiary may, at times, absorb exchange losses for the benefit of the whole. On the other hand, the decentralized approach gives each subsidiary greater control over its exposure, thereby making it better off as a unit. In opting for such a strategy, however, the organization as a whole may find itself placing unnecessary hedges. Chapter 3 illustrates the centralized approach to hedging.

WHY HEDGE?

Hedging activity has largely been influenced by three factors: (1) exchange rate volatility, (2) expanding international trade, and (3) changes in accounting standards.

Volatility

Exchange rates have grown more volatile in recent years. A case in point is the deutsche mark over the 1983 and early 1984 period. Figure 1.1 shows 1983's year-long record-breaking decline that resulted in the deutsche mark losing nearly 22 percent of its value relative to the dollar. Then in January 1984 the deutsche mark rebounded, posting a 10.5 percent gain in just over a month. Following this dramatic upsurge, the deutsche mark fell again. This time the deutsche mark tumbled nearly 19 percent. Caught unprotected, moves of this speed and magnitude can severely damage or even eliminate one's margin of profit.

A volatility study covering the years 1976 through 1985 for the five major currencies (deutsche mark, Canadian dollar, Swiss franc, British pound, and Japanese yen) traded on the International Money Market (IMM) in Chicago confirms the volatility problem. The results are included in Appendix 6 and summarized in the following section. For the study, the quarterly high/low exchange rate range was found for each currency. Rates are expressed in dollars per foreign currency unit. On average, the Swiss franc emerged most volatile (11.2 percent per quarter) followed by the Japanese yen, deutsche mark, British pound, and finally the Canadian dollar. The Canadian dollar's 3.4 percent average quarterly range is significantly lower than the other four. However, the Canadian dollar usually tracks the U.S. dollar, explaining the lower figure. A closer look at the study reveals that currency values at times varied by as much as 25 percent in a three-month period. It is precisely this sort of volatility that has forced corporations and traders to develop methods to protect their foreign currency interests. The techniques of Chapter 3 are a gathering of the protective measures of past and present hedgers. The chapters within Part 2 describe how to harness this volatility and allow it to work for rather than against the hedger.

Trade Growth

Trade between nations is accelerating. The emergence of new nations boasting more efficient production facilities and a unique work ethic has heightened trade competition. Consequently, the

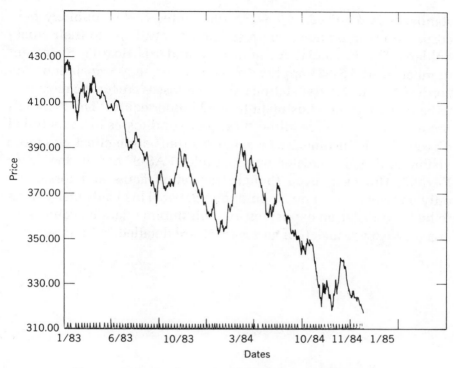

Figure 1.1. Deutsche mark volatility over 1983 and 1984.

bulk of world trade is no longer confined to a handful of industrial giants. Industrial and technological advances have opened doors between some countries and created an interdependency between others. The past decade has also been one of economic upheaval for some nations and prosperity for others. Political environments have shown rapid change. Combined, these factors have created a complicated international business environment beset with uncertainty. As brokers, traders, and businesses react to trade, economic, and political events, their opinions are reflected in the exchange rates. The hedger must be alert to these changes and be ready to incorporate them into the hedging program.

Accounting Standards

The reporting of year end results via financial statements is a necessity for most companies, and the use of professional accounting standards is required by law. In the United States, publicly held corporations must make these statements available to their stockholders. The Financial Accounting Standards Board's Statement number 52 (FAS-52) applies to foreign currency translation. According to FAS-52, translation gains and losses are for the most part to be treated as an adjustment to stockholder equity. The FAS-52's predecessor, FAS-8, required these gains and losses to be included directly in net income. The accounting translation effect was more visible and had a greater impact under FAS-8 than it does with FAS-52. However, even though translation gains and losses are only on paper, they appear on public paper. This leads many firms to hedge translation exposures for their public relations value. Foreign currency translation and FAS-52 are detailed in Chapter 2.

2

Exposure

Stephanie, our sister and daughter, is well known for skipping the details. A "straight-A" student, we once found her trying to light a large log in the fireplace with a single match. Stephanie never did learn to use the tools of fire starting. (Today, she owns a gas grill.)

It's the same with exposure management. One must learn to use the tools. Even the finest exposure management program is of little value until it is first understood what and how much must be hedged. Recognizing where exposure occurs is the critical first step. Isolating the extent of the exposure is the second. This chapter is presented for the hedger desiring a general background in foreign exchange exposure and its measurement. The objective of this chapter is to focus on the basics. A discussion of exposure is presented, followed by a general description of how taxes affect the hedger's position. The balance of the chapter reviews how to measure exposure created by foreign exchange transactions and translation. The net exposure method is introduced as a practical method for measuring exposure within all areas of the corporation. Special attention is given to the impact of currency fluctuation on the firm's financial statements and cash position.

EXPOSURE DEFINED

Perhaps the best place to start is to define the different types of exposure that may confront a businessperson. These are transaction, translation, and economic exposure. The corporate treasurer concerned with the effects of exchange rate fluctuations on current period cash flows is interested in transaction exposure. Translation exposure measures the accounting impact of such fluctuations, while economic exposure takes a longer term cash flow view. However, it is important to remember that transaction, translation, and economic exposure overlap to some degree. For instance, translation adjustments are, in part, a reflection of various transaction exposures over the fiscal year. And today's transaction exposures contribute to the calculation of economic exposure.

Transaction Exposure

Transaction exposure is defined as the potential impact on current period cash flows created by fluctuating exchange rates between one's home currency and the currency in which the transaction is denominated. Every firm with current foreign currency denominated transactions (receivables, payables, loans, etc.) has transaction exposure. A change in the value of the foreign currency alters the value of foreign currency cash flows, once they are measured in the local currency. For example, suppose a U.S. firm agrees to purchase a piece of equipment from a company in West Germany. Payment is to be in deutsche marks. If the value of the deutsche mark rises between the contract date and the date of payment, the marks, which must be purchased in the spot market using dollars, become more expensive. As a result, the West German equipment is suddenly more expensive than was expected and the U.S. firm incurs a cash flow loss. (An example can be found in Chapter 9.) Transaction exposure occurs at both the parent and subsidiary levels. Country taxation affects both entities in differing ways, as later subsections point out.

Contingent Exposure. An extension of transaction risk that is often overlooked concerns potential foreign exchange transactions that are known but have not yet materialized. This type of risk, known as "contingent" exposure, is also a real transaction risk to the firm. Contingent exposure can be illustrated in the bidding on projects that are denominated in a foreign currency. The bid, and implicitly the firm's profit margin, is based on the exchange rates as they are perceived when the proposal is submitted. Months may go by before the contract is awarded. Time creates uncertainty. Exchange rate fluctuations over the evaluation period can cause serious planning problems. The firm ultimately receiving the contract would clearly like to have been hedged over the evaluation period. On the other hand, those firms not receiving the contract, in retrospect, would not need to be hedged. However, since firms cannot know beforehand whether or not they will get the bid, they do have a hedging problem. Chapter 3 shows how foreign currency options are useful for managing such contingent risks.

Translation Exposure

Translation exposure appears when the multinational corporation consolidates the financial statements of all of its foreign subsidiaries with the parent company. All items must be translated into the home (and/or reporting) currency. Should a currency depreciate or appreciate between consolidation dates, items translated at current rates are vulnerable to exchange rate fluctuation. Those translated historically are not. For example, suppose the financial officer of the British subsidiary of a U.S. multinational is evaluating the subsidiary's year end financial statements. The statements show that over the course of the year the subsidiary has maintained an average net asset position equal to 3 million British pounds (BP). The dollar value of the pound has fallen from $1.50 to $1.40 over the same time period. Translation into U.S. dollars reduces the value of the net asset position from $4.5 million to $4.2 million. The result is a $300,000 loss to the parent company.

Translation and FAS-52. Through its FAS rulings, the Financial Accounting Standards Board (FASB) sets guidelines on how U.S. corporations are to report foreign currency accounts in their financial statements. In the United States the appropriate translation rate and methodology depend on two factors: (1) the functional currency and (2) the accounting translation method used. It is important to note that the discussion of foreign currency translation primarily applies to U.S. based corporations.

The Concept of Functional Currency. Under the old FAS-8 rules, translation exposures and related gains and losses directly affected net income, creating wide variations in corporate profit and loss statements. In December 1981, the FASB revised these rules by adopting FAS-52, "Foreign Currency Translation." Under the new rules, each subsidiary is required to measure its books in the "functional currency" prior to translation into the parent currency. FAS-52 defines the functional currency as the primary currency that the subsidiary uses in its day-to-day business.[1] For instance, if a U.S. firm's wholly owned Japanese subsidiary generally uses the yen in its daily operations, the yen would probably be considered the functional currency. On the other hand, a European subsidiary that commonly handles a wide variety of currencies can easily face a confusing situation. When the functional currency is not obvious there are several factors that can aid in its determination. These are addressed in a summary of FAS-52, found in Appendix 1.

Accounting Translation Methods. The appropriate accounting translation method depends on whether the functional currency of the subsidiary is determined to be the U.S. dollar or a foreign currency. If the functional currency is the U.S. dollar, the subsidiary is viewed as merely an outstretched arm of the parent company and not an independent entity. The translation of foreign statements, therefore, proceeds in the same manner as was directed by FAS-8, that is, translation using the temporal accounting method. Under the temporal method, assets and liabilities are translated at differing exchange rates and all gains and losses are recognized in current income. On the other hand, if the functional currency is determined to be a foreign currency the current accounting method is generally used (unless the firm meets specific FASB criteria in which case the temporal method is used). Under the current method, all assets and liabilities are translated at the current rate (the rate prevailing on the consolidation date or some average over the period).

Translation gains and losses are no longer included in net income but are instead treated as an adjustment to stockholder equity. Thus, compared with FAS-8, FAS-52 tends to reduce variations in net income.

Economic Exposure

Transaction and translation exposure recognize only the current impact of exchange rate movements. Economic exposure considers the effect of currency fluctuation on the discounted value of both the current and future cash flows of the firm. Rodriguez[2] defines economic exposure as the gain or loss in the value of the firm from a movement in exchange rates. Calculating exposure in this context requires estimating the effects of exchange rate fluctuations on the firm's current and future product/market areas and investment decisions. This quickly becomes a complicated task that is highly firm specific.

Economic Exposure Determinants.   Suppose that a currency undergoes a substantial decline in value over a short time period, as in a controlled government devaluation. In fact, such an event did occur on September 23, 1985, with the coordinated intervention by the "G-five" to weaken the U.S. dollar. The agreement among the central banks of Japan, West Germany, the United Kingdom, France, and the United States to intervene in the foreign exchange market by selling dollars effectively devalued the dollar 5 percent in a single day. Figure 2.1 shows the sudden appreciation in the value of the Japanese yen (and, therefore, depreciation in the dollar) caused by such intervention.

Donald Kemp[3] provides an interesting summary of the factors that influence economic exposure. Portions of Kemp's observations are included in the following lists. The corporation analyzing its exposure from an economic perspective may take the following points into consideration:

Price Levels

1. Does inflation occur due to the devaluation?
2. How are the firm's costs of production affected?
3. How are foreign prices affected? How much does the firm rely on foreign supplies?
4. How much can the firm alter its sales prices to cope with changing price levels?
5. Will the government impose price controls?

Sales Volume

1. What impact on volume is attributed to the devaluation?
2. What is the impact on the volume due to price level adjustments?

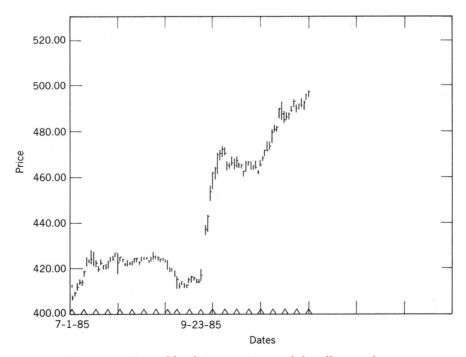

Figure 2.1. Central bank intervention and the effect on the yen.

Timing

1. Immediate or lagged—Will price and volume reactions occur immediately or will there be an adjustment period? If so, how long?

Measuring exposure from an economic perspective is complicated by two factors: First, there are many potential price and volume reactions to a given exchange rate change. Many values must be estimated. Thus economic measurements involve a considerable degree of subjectivity and uncertainty. Second, evaluating the overall performance is normally levied from an accounting standpoint, not an economic one. Firm performance is reflected through the year-end financial accounting statements. Consequently, business decisions are often based on how the results will look through the eyes of the stockholder. Likewise, managers are usually evaluated on an accounting basis. Business decisions that are economically better for the firm may be brushed aside because of their accounting effects.

Theoretically, economic exposure is perhaps the most accurate method for determining the real impact exchange rate changes have on the value of the firm. Unfortunately, measuring the economic impact becomes so difficult and subjective that managers generally choose accounting methods.

After-Tax Exposure

When it comes to measuring and protecting exposure, taxes play their usual role—they complicate things. Still, it is critical that all tax effects be included in the equation. The resulting foreign exchange gains and losses are often subject to taxation by local authorities. (Note that translated balance sheet items are not generally taxed, but transactional hedges against them may be.) After-tax exposure recognizes the tax effects of foreign currency transactions and/or the translation of foreign currency accounts.

Hedging exposure after taxes (vs. before tax) helps to avoid unnecessary hedge costs that may be caused by hedging the wrong

TABLE 2.1.   BEFORE-TAX VS. AFTER-TAX EXPOSURE AND
             EXCHANGE RATE EFFECTS

	Before-Tax		After-Tax	
	Exposure	Hedge	Exposure	Hedge
Exposure (FC)	100,000	100,000	60,000	60,000
Initial $ value	100,000	100,000	60,000	60,000
Final $ value	90,000	110,000	54,000	66,000
Exchange G/L ($)	(10,000)	10,000	(6,000)	6,000
Tax effect (.40)	4,000	(4,000)	—	—
Net exchange G/L	(6,000)	6,000	(6,000)	6,000
G/L on hedge	0		0	

amount or in the wrong currency. For example, a U.S. manufacturer has foreign currency (FC) receivables totaling FC 100,000. Assume also that foreign exchange gains and losses are subject to a 40
percent tax rate. In effect, 40 percent of the receivable goes to taxes.
After taxes, only 60 percent of the receivable, or FC 60,000, is actually exposed. Thus, only 60 percent needs to be hedged.

To show the effect of taxation, consider two hedges that the manufacturer might place. The first covers the exposure measured
before taxes are considered, and the second after taxes. Table 2.1
summarizes the results. The before-tax hedge equals FC 100,000
while the after-tax hedge comes to FC 60,000. Suppose that foreign
currency depreciates 10 percent, from FC 1.0 = $1.0 to FC 1.0 =
$0.9. From a before-tax perspective, the dollar value of the expo-
sure has declined from $100,000 to $90,000. This $10,000 foreign
exchange loss is offset by a $10,000 foreign exchange gain on the
hedge. The tax effects on the exchange gains and losses (G/L) offset
each other as well, resulting in no net change in the manufacturer's
position. On the other hand, if calculated from an after-tax viewpoint the loss on the "after-tax" exposure is $6,000. The offsetting
gain on the hedge leaves the manufacturer neutral.

Table 2.1 shows that hedging either before taxes or after taxes
equally covers the exposure. However, if the firm is aware of its tax
position prior to initiating the hedge, hedging the smaller (after-
tax) amount may significantly reduce hedge costs.

Consolidated After-Tax Exposure. Multinationals with foreign subsidiaries are faced with a "two-tiered" exposure situation. First, a foreign subsidiary's transactions with other countries create exposure in the subsidiary's local currency (the currency of the subsidiary's host country). Second, any exposure to the subsidiary represents an indirect exposure to the parent. And as usual, the differing tax systems further complicate matters. Consolidated after-tax exposure recognizes transaction and translation exposure from an after-tax viewpoint.

Take the case of a subsidiary with a receivable in a third currency (a currency other than the subsidiary's local currency or the parent currency). The subsidiary is subject to a 40 percent tax rate. What initially appears to be an exposure to the parent in the third currency actually emerges as two exposures in two different currencies.

1. *The Subsidiary Transaction Tax Effect.* Foreign exchange gains and losses on the subsidiary's receivable are taxed by local authorities at the 40 percent rate. Thus, 40 percent of the receivable is exposed in the subsidiary's local currency.

2. *Parent Translation Exposure.* The remaining 60 percent is not taxed and retains its value in the third currency. Since foreign currency translation is generally not a tax event, the full 60 percent represents a parent translation exposure in the third currency. Figure 2.2 illustrates this two-tiered exposure situation.

Consolidated after-tax exposure separates the pre-tax exposure into two distinct after-tax exposures, each subject to different exchange rates and tax codes. (After-tax exposure is reviewed further in Chapter 4.)

MEASURING EXPOSURE: ACCOUNTING VERSUS CASH FLOW

Company objectives ultimately dictate how exposure is measured and subsequently hedged. Companies interested in measuring the impact of currency movements on their balance sheets will likely use an accounting approach. Those monitoring the cash impact

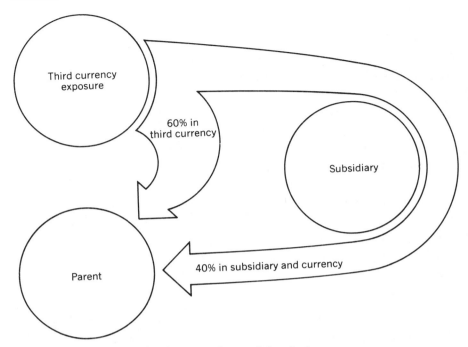

Figure 2.2. The division of consolidated after-tax exposure.

measure their exposure from a cash-flow perspective. Often companies measure and hedge using both approaches. That is, companies commonly hedge individual foreign exchange transactions
(cash) throughout the year. These same firms (or their parents),
however, may also be hedging projected balance sheet figures (accounting) to assure favorable year-end statements.

It is important to keep in mind that cash-flow exposure often differs from accounting exposure. The results of hedging one can directly affect the other. Hedging cash flow exposure to reduce potential transaction losses may lead to accounting losses. Conversely,
hedging accounting exposure may produce an accounting gain on
the exposure and a cash loss on the hedge.[4] For example, suppose
that a manufacturer has a net liability in a foreign currency. An appreciation of the foreign currency relative to the manufacturer's
home currency will cause the liability to grow. The firm hedges by
purchasing a forward contract in the exposed currency (see Chap-

ter 3 for an explanation of forward contracts). Once the hedge is placed, there are three possible scenarios:

1. *The Foreign Currency Appreciates*

   A rise in the value of the foreign currency produces an accounting loss on the liability and a cash-flow gain on the forward contract.

2. *The Foreign Currency Depreciates*

   A devalued foreign currency produces an accounting gain on the liability and a cash loss on the forward contract.

3. *No Change in Relative Currency Values Occurs*

   There are no gains or losses on either side.

The accounting effects are on paper, but gains and losses on the forward contract directly affect the company's cash position. In short, the cash-flow approach measures the effects of currency fluctuations in the exposed currency, while the accounting method evaluates exposure relative to the currency of the parent company. Thus, there is no cash-flow impact if the exposed currency does not change relative to the local currency. And there is no accounting effect if the exposed currency does not change relative to the parent currency.[5] The following section presents more examples of this kind.

Measuring Exposure in Current Accounts

The current accounts, that is, receivables, payables, and so on, are clearly the most visible areas affected by fluctuating exchange rates. These are the firm's monetary assets and/or liabilities denominated in foreign currency. This section identifies exposure in current accounts and the nature of the transactions that produce it. The net exposure approach to measuring current account exposure is explained and illustrated. The focus is on measurement from a centralized perspective, since its parts are directly applicable to a decentralized approach.

It is important to note that the current accounts are not the only exposure victims. Exposure surfaces in the intercompany, inventory, fixed asset, and long-term debt areas too. Later sections of this chapter identify these exposures.

Measuring exposure from any perspective requires that two fundamental questions be answered. First, where did the exposure originate? On the parent level or the subsidiary level? And second, in what currency is the exposure denominated? While this latter question appears to have many potential answers, in terms of measuring exposure there are only a few. If it is the parent that enters into a transaction, three currency types may be involved:

1. The parent can deal in its own currency. These transactions do not constitute an exposure problem, since no exposure is created.
2. The parent can deal in a subsidiary's currency (SC). This represents an exposure to the parent in SC.
3. Or, the parent can transact in a third currency (TC); that is, a currency other than its own or that of a subsidiary. Transactions in third currencies expose the parent in TC.

Likewise, subsidiaries undertake transactions in the following currency types:

1. The subsidiary might deal in its own currency (SC). While these transactions do not expose the subsidiary, the parent is exposed in SC.

TABLE 2.2.   EXPOSURE TRANSACTION TYPES

A. Parent transactions denominated in foreign currency (SC or TC)
B. Subsidiary transactions denominated in the subsidiary's currency (SC)
C. Subsidiary transactions denominated in a third currency (TC)
D. Subsidiary transactions denominated in the parent's currency (PC)

2. The subsidiary can deal in the parent currency (PC). These transactions by themselves do not create exposure at the parent level, but their tax effects do. Subsidiary revenues and expenses are taxed in the subsidiary currency, thereby exposing the parent in SC.

3. The subsidiary can transact in TC. These transactions create exposures for both the subsidiary and the parent.

Both the origin and denomination of the currency play an important role in accurately measuring exposure. Table 2.2 summarizes the types of transactions that influence exposure at the parent level.

Once the origin and denomination are understood, it is just a matter of applying the appropriate equation to measure the exposure. The net exposure approach handles this seemingly complicated problem neatly and concisely.

The Net Exposure Method. This method calculates net after-tax exposure from the pre-tax exposure by applying one of four equations, depending on the transaction involved (see Table 2.2). Each formula accounts for the taxable portion of the exposure and the exchange rates that apply to each situation. The final product is the net after-tax exposure for a specific currency. To measure net exposures properly the answers to the following questions must first be found:

1. What is the initial exposure (before taxes)?
2. Does taxation apply?
3. What currency are we dealing in?

Table 2.3 contains the equations that are used to measure both the net accounting and net cash-flow exposures for each transaction listed in Table 2.2. Multiplying the pre-tax exposure (X) for each transaction by the appropriate formula gives the net after-tax exposure. Equations B, C, and D measure exposure in the subsidiary's currency. Equation A calculates exposure in a foreign currency other than the SC. Finally, once the net exposure has been

TABLE 2.3.   NET EXPOSURE FORMULAS FOR ACCOUNTING AND CASH-FLOW EXPOSURE

	Formula	
Transaction	Accounting	Cash Flow
A. Prnt Trans in FC	$X*(1 - \text{prnt tax})$	$X*(1 - \text{prnt tax})$
B. Subs Trans in SC	X = After-tax exposure	No exposure
C. Subs Trans in TC	Exposures in two currencies: $TC = X*(1 - \text{subs tax})$ $SC = X*(\text{TC/SC})$ (subs tax)	Exposures in two currencies: $TC = X*(1 - \text{subs tax})$ $SC = -X*(\text{TC/SC})$ $(1 - \text{subs tax})$
D. Subs Trans in PC	$X*(\text{subs tax})/SC$	$X*(1 - \text{subs tax})/SC$

Note: "X" equals pre-tax exposure, "$*$" indicates multiplication (multiplication is implied between two parentheses), all exchange rates (SC, TC, etc.) are spot rates when the exposure is initiated, and "tax" represents the tax rate (40% for all examples).

calculated, the net after-tax gain or loss can be determined. This is found by multiplying the net exposure by the change in the exchange rate over the period.

The obvious advantage to using this method is its ease. But understanding how the exposure is derived, and why, is vitally important. Close attention is paid to the hows and whys in the following subsections, which illustrate the calculation of exposure for each of the situations described in Table 2.3. All examples use a

TABLE 2.4.   EXCHANGE RATES FOR ALL ILLUSTRATIONS

Time	Exchange Rates
t_0	PC 1.0 = SC 1.0 = TC 1.0
t_1	SC 1.0 = PC 1.1 TC 1.0 = PC 0.9 TC 1.0 = SC 0.82

standard set of exchange rates for the PC, SC, and TC. These are found in Table 2.4.

At time t_0 all currencies are equal. By time t_1, SC has appreciated relative to PC, and TC has depreciated against both PC and SC.

Parent Transactions in Foreign Currency. The parent company assumes exposure any time it has foreign exchange transactions denominated in a currency other than its own (PC). Suppose a manufacturer sells equipment to a firm in another country (or possibly to one of its foreign subsidiaries). The sale is contracted in the currency of the other country (TC). According to the exchange rates listed in Table 2.4, on the contract date (t_0) all currencies have equal value. If the equipment is priced at TC 100,000, the manufacturer's pre-tax exposure is TC 100,000. In terms of the parent currency, the equipment is valued at PC 100,000.

ACCOUNTING EXPOSURE. The net after-tax accounting exposure is found by using equation A from Table 2.3:

$$\text{Pre-tax exposure} * (1 - \text{parent tax})^* \quad \text{(A, Table 2.3)}$$

Given that the tax rate for all examples is assumed to be 40 percent, the net after-tax accounting exposure to the manufacturer is:

$$\text{TC } 100,000 * (1 - .40)$$
$$\text{or, TC } 60,000$$

CASH-FLOW EXPOSURE. In the case of parent transactions in foreign currency, the net after-tax cash-flow exposure mirrors the accounting exposure. Because parent foreign currency transactions create genuine exposures (not translation items), gains and losses on these transactions are taxable. Any gain or loss on these transactions directly affects the cash flow of the firm.

COMPUTING GAINS AND LOSSES. Continuing with the previous example, suppose that three months pass (t_1) before the manufac-

---

*Note that asterisks represent multiplication signs throughout.

turer delivers the equipment and receives the TC 100,000 as payment for its efforts. The exchange rate between the two countries has since changed. The third currency is no longer worth PC 1.0. Instead, it has depreciated by 0.1 to PC 0.9. When the manufacturer exchanges the TC 100,000 for home currency it receives only PC 90,000.

ACCOUNTING GAIN/LOSS. The net after-tax exposure gain or loss (G/L) is found by multiplying the net accounting exposure by the change in the exchange rate (ER).

$$\text{Net G/L} = \text{Net exposure} * (\text{ERt}_1 - \text{ERt}_0) \qquad (2.1)$$
$$= \text{TC } 60,000 * (0.9 - 1.0)$$
$$= - \text{PC } 6,000$$

The PC 6,000 loss can be explained another way:

1. Between t_0 and t_1, the manufacturer loses PC 10,000 to exchange rate fluctuation (100,000 − 90,000).
2. The manufacturer receives a PC 4,000 tax credit on the loss.
3. The net loss after tax is, therefore, PC 6,000.

Subsidiary Transactions in Subsidiary Currency. This time, assume the equipment manufacturer of the previous example is a foreign subsidiary of the parent. The same sale is made locally rather than to a third country and the price tag is SC 100,000. In effect, the subsidiary has made the sale to another firm in the subsidiary's host country. From the standpoint of the parent, the equipment is initially valued at PC 100,000 (PC 1 = SC 1). The subsidiary is not exposed to transaction risk in its own currency. However, these transactions may create an exposure to the parent on translation.

ACCOUNTING EXPOSURE. The after-tax accounting exposure created by such transactions equals the pre-tax exposure, or SC 100,000 (see equation B, Table 2.3). The full amount is considered exposed, because taxes generally do not apply to foreign currency translation.

CASH-FLOW EXPOSURE. In this case the net after-tax cash-flow exposure is zero. Since the sale originates at the subsidiary level (locally), exchange rate fluctuations do not affect the subsidiary's cash position.

COMPUTING GAINS AND LOSSES. Suppose that it is now time t_1 and the SC has appreciated relative to the PC. SC 1.0 now buys PC 1.1. The SC appreciation does not create a cash-flow gain or loss, as the sale was denominated locally. However, the translation of the receivable into the parent currency does have an accounting impact.

ACCOUNTING GAIN/LOSS. Multiplying the net accounting exposure by the change in exchange rates:

$$\text{Net G/L} = \text{net exposure} * (\text{ERt}_1 - \text{ERt}_0) \qquad (2.2)$$
$$= \text{SC } 100{,}000 * (1.1 - 1.0)$$
$$= \text{PC } 10{,}000$$

The parent records a translation gain totaling PC 10,000.

Subsidiary Transactions Denominated in a Third Currency. Suppose the subsidiary sells the equipment to a buyer in a third country and invoices the sale in the third country's currency (TC 100,000). It was pointed out earlier that transactions of this sort result in exposures in two currencies, the third currency and the subsidiary's currency. Equations C of Table 2.3 calculate the net exposures for these transactions.

ACCOUNTING EXPOSURE. Gains and losses on the receivable (in TC) are subject to taxation at the subsidiary level (in SC). Thus, the taxable portion (40 percent) represents an exposure to the parent in SC. The remaining 60 percent represents a translation exposure to the parent in TC.

In third currency:
= Pre-tax exposure * (1 − subsidiary tax rate)
or, TC 60,000

In subsidiary currency:
= Pre-tax exposure * (TC/SC) (subsidiary tax rate)
= TC 100,000 * (1.0/1.0) (.40)
or, SC 40,000

CASH-FLOW EXPOSURE. Cash-flow exposure also appears in two currencies: TC and SC. Exchange rate fluctuation between the TC and the SC alters the value to the TC receivable, thereby directly affecting the subsidiary's cash position. Again, due to subsidiary taxation, 60 percent of the receivable is exposed in TC. Assuming eventual repatriation to the parent, the receivable carried on the subsidiary's books represents a cash-flow exposure to the parent in SC.

In third currency:
= Pre-tax exposure * (1 − parent tax rate)
= TC 100,000 * (1 − .40)
or, TC 60,000

In subsidiary currency:
= − Pre-tax exposure * (TC/SC)(1 − subsidiary tax rate)
= − TC 100,000 * (1.0/1.0) (1 − .40)
or, − SC 60,000

COMPUTING GAINS AND LOSSES

Accounting

In third currency:
= Net exposure * $(ERt_1 − ERt_0)$
= TC 60,000 * (0.9 − 1.0)
or, − PC 6,000

Plus, in subsidiary currency:
= SC 40,000 * (1.1 − 1.0)
or, PC 4000

Adding these two figures gives a net accounting loss of PC 2,000.

Cash Flow

> In third currency:
> = Net exposure $*$ $(ERt_1 - ERt_0)$
> = TC 60,000 $*$ $(0.9 - 1.0)$
> or, $-$ PC 6,000
>
> Plus, in subsidiary currency:
> $-$ SC 60,000 $*$ $(1.1 - 1.0)$
> or, $-$ PC 6,000

In total, the subsidiary incurs a cash-flow loss of PC 12,000. Two events are responsible for this loss. First, the subsidiary loses PC 6,000 to TC/SC exchange rate fluctuation. And second, the subsidiary loses an additional PC 6,000 to PC/SC fluctuation. While this latter loss is reflected as a translation gain to the parent, it is a cash-flow loss to the subsidiary.

Subsidiary Transactions Denominated in Parent Currency.   An inter-company account transaction is used for this illustration. Inter-company accounts are often ignored as an exchange risk item. The reasoning is that the translation of these accounts nets zero on a pre-tax basis. The parent's loss is the subsidiary's gain and vice versa. It should be noted that this is only true from an accounting perspective, and once taxes are considered it is not true at all.

Suppose a foreign subsidiary manufactures the equipment and sells it to the parent company. The subsidiary invoices the sale in the parent currency, and thus carries on its books a receivable from the parent for PC 100,000.

ACCOUNTING EXPOSURE.   Since the receivable is in the parent currency, changes in exchange rates do not directly affect the parent company. They do, however, impact the subsidiary, as foreign exchange gains and losses are a tax event by the subsidiary's host country. In turn, the subsidiary's tax or tax credit creates an exposure to the parent in the subsidiary's currency. Using formula D of Table 2.3, net accounting exposure:

= Pre-tax exposure $*$ (subsidiary tax rate)/SC
= PC 100,000 $*$ (.40)/1.0
or, SC 40,000

CASH-FLOW EXPOSURE.   The net cash-flow exposure represents the portion directly affecting the subsidiary's cash position:

= Pre-tax exposure $*$ (1 $-$ subsidiary tax rate)/SC
= PC 100,000 (1 $-$ .40)/1.0
or, SC 60,000

COMPUTING GAINS AND LOSSES

Accounting

= Net exposure $*$ (ERt$_1$ $-$ ERt$_0$)
= SC 40,000 $*$ (1.1 $-$ 1.0)
or, PC 4,000

Cash Flow

= SC 60,000 $*$ (1.1 $-$ 1.0)
or, PC 6,000

The PC 4,000 accounting gain reflects the tax on the foreign exchange gain paid by the subsidiary. Conversely, the PC 6,000 cash-flow gain represents the net of the tax paid by the subsidiary.

Exposure in Inventory

Measuring inventory exposure is similar to measuring exposure in current accounts and occurs whenever a firm sells inventory abroad, holds inventory to be sold abroad, or buys inventory denominated in foreign currency and sells it locally.[6] Fluctuating exchange rates influence the value of inventory. Changing inventory values ultimately result in or contribute to a translation adjustment on the consolidation of the firm's financial statements. Actual exposure values will differ from firm to firm, depending on the accounting rules for inventory valuation that are followed by each firm (last-in, first-out; first-in, first-out; lower of cost or market, etc.).

Income Statement Exposure

If the parent's and/or its subsidiary's revenues and expenses are denominated in foreign currency, these areas are also exposed to currency fluctuation. If the exchange rate between the foreign currency and the parent currency changes during the period of exposure, the parent currency equivalent of the revenues and expenses will change too. These changes produce translation gains and losses for the reporting unit. Again, measuring the impact of exchange rate fluctuation depends on the origin (parent or subsidiary) and on the currency denomination (PC, SC, or TC). Measurement proceeds much in the same way as the current account illustrations described previously. Translation gains and losses in income are not usually reported as foreign exchange gains and losses; rather, they are treated as an *operating variance* affecting net income. Revenues and expenses do, however, generate assets and liabilities, and net assets generated may affect the translation adjustment of the reporting unit.[7]

Fixed Assets

Fixed assets are a delicate item in terms of measuring accounting exposure. The translation of fixed assets depends on the accounting method used in the translation process. If the functional currency is a foreign currency the current rate method is used. Otherwise, if the functional currency is the U.S. dollar the historical rate is used (see Table 1, Appendix 1). Throughout the life of the asset, each method will produce different exposure values. The current method recognizes gains and losses from changing rates in each period; thus, the asset is exposed from period to period. Under the historical method these gains and losses are deferred until the asset is sold. Measuring exposure in fixed assets is further complicated by depreciation expenses. Depreciation creates exposure when the current method is used for translation. Foreign exchange gains and losses arising from the translation of depreciation expense items are accounting gains and losses. They do not affect cash flow.

In the final analysis, using either the current or the historical method for translation yields the same results. Their principal difference stems from when foreign exchange gains and losses are recognized—immediately or on the sale of the asset.

Although fixed assets do not directly affect cash flow, they are revenue generating. These revenues may in turn be exposed to exchange rate fluctuation.

Long-Term Debt

According to FAS-52, long-term debt is to be translated at the current exchange rate regardless of whether the functional currency is a foreign currency or the U.S. dollar. Consequently, exchange rate changes over the fiscal year may contribute to translation gains and losses (adjustments). Because most long-term debt remains on the company's books through the current period, accounting for such debt using the "current" method has led to considerable debate. Over the life of the debt, exchange rates may rise, fall, rise, and so on. Foreign exchange gains over one year are often erased by losses over the next. A number of alternatives have been suggested.[8] These range from deferring the translation gains and/or losses produced by current rate reporting until the debt matures, to recognizing only the current portion immediately and deferring the rest.

Nonetheless, long-term debt does represent an exposure to the firm. If the exchange rate of today has declined relative to its rate of five years ago, foreign debt contracted five years ago will be more expensive to repay today (in parent currency). In most cases, yearly interest expenses must be recognized. These payments are known and also exposed.

NOTES

1. FASB Statement no. 52, "Foreign Currency Translation," para. 5, 1981.
2. For a thorough analysis on economic exposure, see Rodriguez, Rita M. "Measuring and Controlling Multinational's Exchange Risk." *Financial Analysts Journal* (Nov.–Dec. 1979): 49–55.

3. Much of the material in this section is drawn from Kemp, Donald S. "The Attraction of Rule 52." *Euromoney* (November 1982): 167–174.

4. George, Abraham M., *Foreign Exchange Management of the Multinational*. New York: Praeger, 1978, 87ff.

5. *Ibid.*

6. Antl, B. (ed.). *Currency Risk and the Corporation*. London: *Euromoney* (1981): 36ff.

7. *Ibid.*

8. *Ibid.*; Rodriguez, Rita M. "Measuring and Controlling Multinational's Exchange Risk." *Financial Analysts Journal* (Nov.–Dec. 1979): 49–55; Antl, Boris, ed. *The Management of Foreign Exchange Risk*. London: *Euromoney* (1980): 28.

3

Hedging: Managing Exposure

$\mathbf{C}$hapters 1 and 2 detailed the origin of currency exposure and its measurement; they also demonstrated the effect of exchange rate fluctuation on the calculated exposure value. Like billiards, where there are many combinations of hits and several pockets in which to sink a ball, the options are numerous when it comes to achieving currency protection. This chapter examines over 20 techniques used by hedgers to protect and manage their exposure given potential changes in the value of the underlying currency.

Hedging techniques may be implemented either internally or externally. Managing exposure internally entails using sources within the firm to hedge foreign exchange risk. Balance sheet manipulation, pricing policies, and so forth fall into this area. External methods are those that require the hedger to venture outside the organization for aid in protecting exposure. These include bank forward foreign exchange contracts, currency futures and options, and other instruments.

It is virtually impossible to limit this complex and expanding area to a single chapter. A few volumes would be more appropriate, and some are already available. Thus our coverage is not intended to be exhaustive. Rather, it is meant to provide a practical understanding of the most significant methods and to serve as a guide to the work of others.

THE PROCESS

Exposure management is the preservation and control of foreign currency denominated assets and liabilities. The term *hedging*, when applied to foreign exchange, is often simply viewed as taking an offsetting currency position in the forward or futures market. But hedging is much more than this. Hedging is a complete process. The process begins with top management recognizing the potential impact currency risk can have on the organization, and then instituting procedures for controlling that risk. Management must decide what type of hedger it wants (and is able) to be. Does the firm want to be conservative or aggressive in its basic approach to hedging? Company philosophy, size and, of course, the types of business and transactions involved all play a critical role in this decision.

Conservative hedgers typically use defensive strategies, such as offsetting known exposures with a forward contract. Here, the principal aim is to break even. Nothing is gained; but more important, little is lost. Aggressive hedgers, on the other hand, use the same techniques as conservative hedgers, but they implement them differently. While protection remains the primary goal, these hedgers also seek to take advantage of potential windfall gains produced by not hedging when the foreign exchange tide is with them. An example of an aggressive hedger is one who intentionally holds payables in currencies that are expected to devalue.

The important difference between conservative and aggressive hedgers is thus not what protective strategies they use, but how they use them. This chapter discusses the methods themselves in the traditional, more conservative context. Chapter 9 discusses how to employ the techniques more aggressively. In fact, the entirety of Part 2 might properly be called the handbook of aggressive hedging.

Hedging Considerations

Often more than one technique may be used to cover a specific exposure. This can create difficulties when the time comes to evaluate and select the hedge that is in the best interest of both the exposure and the firm as a whole. The following five factors serve as basic guidelines to proper hedge selection.

1. *Performance*

The technique must first perform the designated function, that is, protect the exposure.

2. *Cost/Risk*

The hedge must be placed at reasonable cost. If the expected cost is greater than the potential exposure loss, obviously the cost is too high. Ideally the cost will be only a fraction of the potential loss (or as shown in Part 2, sometimes no cost at all).

3. *Time*

The hedge must conform to the exposure period. For example, using a longer-term method, such as long-term borrowing, to hedge a short-term exposure may not be appropriate, even if it is the least expensive. Once the exposure period is over, the long-term borrowing hedge no longer has an exposure to offset and thus becomes an exposure itself.

4. *Flexibility*

The hedge must meet the sensitivity of the exposure it is designed to cover. For instance, consider the manager who protects a contingent future sale (a sale that may or may not materialize) with a binding forward foreign exchange contract. If the sale does not materialize, the firm may end up with a speculative position and be forced to absorb a forward contract loss.

5. *Regulations*

The use of some techniques may be restricted due to specific foreign exchange regulations. Chapter 5 outlines foreign exchange controls placed by the major countries.

These and other points specific to each firm should be carefully considered during the selection of a hedge strategy.

INTERNAL TECHNIQUES

Internal techniques are those methods inside the corporation that are used to neutralize or minimize foreign exchange risk. These strategies take many forms, depending on the extent of exposure coverage and the complexity of the firm's operations. Many take the form of balance sheet adjustments involving the transfer of monetary assets and liabilities into currencies most apt to work in their favor. Others, such as pricing strategies, are akin to *preventative maintenance* policies. Here, the firm designates which currencies it feels are safe to deal in, effectively avoiding potential foreign exchange problems before they occur.

The application of these measures varies from hedger to hedger. The smaller firm, or a company that operates almost entirely on a transaction-by-transaction basis (an import/export firm), probably has limited use for internal measures. Conversely, the larger multinational has a broad spectrum of available techniques from which to choose.

Asset and Liability Adjustments

Monetary assets and liabilities that are denominated in foreign currencies are highly vulnerable to exchange rate fluctuation. Changing currency values have the potential to wipe out profit margins and/or cause liabilities to grow unexpectedly (in home currency terms). Asset and liability management is the careful positioning or transfer of these accounts into currencies that have the highest probability of maintaining or enhancing their value. Holding monetary assets in strong currencies and monetary liabilities in weak currencies is fundamental to this approach. Strong currencies tend to retain or increase in value relative to the home or a base currency. Weak currencies do just the opposite: they tend to lose value over time.

Implementing asset and liability adjustments as a part of normal operations can help the firm maintain a natural hedge against exposure. The use of some techniques such as local currency borrowing (discussed in the following subsection) may be limited or prohibited due to a country's currency controls (see Chapter 5). For others, as in the leading and lagging of payments, it may simply be a matter of setting policy. In any event, employing these strategies often reduces the need for more specific hedging methods such as forward or futures contracting.

Local Currency Borrowing. Multinationals with subsidiaries in countries where the local (subsidiary) currency is expected to devalue can use local currency borrowing to hedge translation exposure. This method is particularly attractive if the subsidiary is simultaneously in need of borrowed funds. The cost of this approach is a function of the firm's borrowing costs.

A case in point: Suppose that a British subsidiary of a U.S. manufacturer has a net asset exposure totaling 1,000,000 British pounds (BP). The current exchange rate is BP 1.00 = $1.60. If the pound devalues, the parent will incur a translation loss upon consolidation of the financial statements. One way to protect against such losses is to assume a liability that offsets the net asset exposure. By borrowing British pounds (the SC) equal to the after-tax exposure, any loss on the exposed asset will be offset by an equal gain on the liability. Thus, the subsidiary borrows BP 1 million for one year at a 10 percent Eurosterling rate (i). Note that the subsidiary does pay interest on the borrowing. Given that the British subsidiary receives a 40 percent deduction on the interest as a business expense, the U.S. manufacturer's pre-tax interest expense exposure is:

1. Interest expense exposure = (1 − subs. tax)*(i) * (loan amount)
   $$= (1 - .4)*(0.10)*(BP\ 1,000,000)$$
   $$= (BP\ 60,000)$$

Including the net asset and local borrowing expense gives the total pre-tax exposure:

2. Net asset exposure   =   BP 1,000,000
3. Local borrowing   =   (BP 1,000,000)

Total pre-tax exposure =   (BP 60,000)
(1) + (2) + (3)

Notice that the sterling borrowing directly offsets the net asset exposure, leaving the interest expense as the only exposed position (one could always consider hedging this exposure also).

NET AFTER-TAX EXPOSURE.   The net exposure method of Chapter 2 is used to determine the transaction and translation effects of the borrowing. Since the interest payments made by the British subsidiary are transactions in its own currency (SC), the net after-tax exposure equals the pre-tax exposure (see Chapter 2, Table 2.3, Equation B).

COMPUTING GAINS AND LOSSES.   A year passes and the pound has fallen from \$1.60 to \$1.50. The subsidiary's interest expense becomes less expensive in dollar terms. The translation gain or loss is found as in Equation 2.1 by multiplying the net exposure by the change in the exchange rate.

$$
\begin{aligned}
\text{G/L} &= \text{Net after-tax exposure} * (\text{ERt}_1 - \text{ERt}_0) \\
&= (\text{BP } 60{,}000) * (1.40 - 1.50) \\
&= \$6{,}000
\end{aligned}
$$

Thus, the local currency hedge results in a \$6,000 translation gain to the U.S. manufacturer. There is no gain or loss on the exposure itself, since all losses on the net asset position were compensated by equal gains on the borrowing.

It is important to note that this hedge did cost the subsidiary BP 60,000 in after-tax interest charges. When evaluating these types of hedges, the subsidiary's financial position must be considered. After all, it is the subsidiary that bears most of the cost.

SECONDARY EFFECTS.   Hedging techniques that rely on borrowing are exposed to more than just exchange rate risk. They are also subject to interest rate risk. While this risk may be small in comparison to that of potential exchange rate fluctuation, it should not be ignored completely. Interest rate risk increases with the size of the borrowing. And like exchange rates, interest rates have grown more volatile in recent years.

Local currency borrowing is frequently used by multinationals with subsidiaries stationed in weak currency countries. Frequently the interest rates within these countries are considerably higher. High interest expenses must be weighed against the cost of borrowing alternative currencies or the use of another strategy.

Leading and Lagging.   Leading and lagging is the intentional speeding up or slowing down of payables and/or receivables, based on exchange rate forecasts and corresponding rates of interest. As a general rule, companies try to accelerate the collection of receivables and delay the payment of payables denominated in currencies expected to depreciate. Conversely, firms lead the payment of payables denominated in currencies expected to appreciate. A "leading" candidate might be a U.S. firm with payables in deutsche marks (DM) that are expected to appreciate over the near term. Paying the debt immediately protects the company from unexpectedly costly deutsche mark expenses (in dollar terms). Because leading may require local currency borrowing to finance the prepayment, steps should be taken to ensure that the cost of borrowing does not exceed the forecasted savings on the exposure.

The lead/lag approach is most effective (and most often used) in conjunction with intercompany transactions. Cooperation from both sides allows the firm to take full advantage of this technique. The intercompany lead/lag decision simply depends on which party can put the funds to better use. Consider the case of a German subsidiary with intercompany payables to its U.S. parent. The subsidiary has the option to either lag payment and invest locally, or borrow locally and lead payment so the parent can invest the funds at home. One procedure[1] used to arrive at such co-op decisions is outlined in the following discussion. The current exchange rate, interest rates within the respective countries, and exchange rate forecasts all play integral roles. First, the current exchange rate and country interest rates are used to find the *break-even* exchange rate (BE_n). The BE_n is the future exchange rate necessary to make the subsidiary indifferent to leading or lagging. Then the break-even rate is compared with company exchange rate forecasts. Based on the relationship between the two rates, the decision to lead or lag is made. The break-even concept in exchange rates is an outgrowth of the interest rate parity (IRP) theory. The IRP theory states that the interest rate differential between two countries' currencies will be reflected in their foreign exchange rates. The IRP will be discussed in further detail later in this chapter.

Equations 3.1 and 3.2 are used to find the break-even point. Here, a and b refer to the countries of the engaged parties, i is the interest rate, n represents the time period in years, and ER_0 is the current exchange rate (the exchange rate at time zero).

$$(1 + i_a)^n = (1 + i_b)^n * (ER_0/BE_n) \qquad (3.1)$$

Or, solving for BE_n:

$$BE_n = [(1 + i_b)^n / (1 + i_a)^n] * ER_0 \qquad (3.2)$$

Assume that the German subsidiary has a three-month ($n = .25$), $100,000 intercompany payable to its U.S. parent. The current exchange rate is DM $1.0 = \$0.40$ and the three-month U.S. interest rate is 12 percent while the rate earned in Germany is 9 percent. The exchange rate three months hence is forecast to be $0.41. The firm needs to determine if the subsidiary should lead or lag payment. (Germany is country a, the U.S. is country b.)

The first order of business is to find the break even exchange rate. Using equation 3.2:

$$BE_n = [(1.12)^{.25} / (1.09)^{.25}] * (0.40)$$
$$BE_n = \$0.4027$$

Put simply, if the exchange rate is expected to be below the break-even point, the subsidiary should lead payment, allowing the funds to be invested in the United States. On the other hand, if the firm expects the exchange rate to move above $0.4027, the subsidiary should lag payment and invest in Germany. Since the forecasted exchange rate is $0.41, the subsidiary should lag payment. The following three cases illustrate the relationship between the break-even point and various other exchange rates. These are:

1. Leading payment at the spot rate
2. Lagging payment until the exchange rate has fallen below the break-even level

3. Lagging payment until the exchange rate has risen above the break-even level

CASE ONE: LEADING AT THE SPOT RATE. Assume that the German subsidiary immediately led payment (when the exchange rate was $0.40) and the parent invested the amount received at the U.S. rate. The net dollar value of the transaction (after three months) is:

$$\$100,000 * (1.12)^{.25} = \$102,873$$

CASE TWO: LAGGING PAYMENT BELOW THE BREAK-EVEN LEVEL. Suppose that the subsidiary did not lead but instead lagged and invested locally, converting the payable into dollars when the exchange rate is $0.39. In this case, the total amount received by the parent is:

$$DM\ 250,000 * (1.09)^{.25} * (0.39)$$
$$= \$99,620$$

CASE THREE: LAGGING PAYMENT ABOVE THE BREAK-EVEN LEVEL. If the exchange rate at the end of the period is $0.41, the amount received by the parent equals:

$$DM\ 250,000 * (1.09)^{.25} * (0.41)$$
$$= \$104,000$$

Table 3.1 includes additional examples of lagging by the subsidiary. Notice that the dollar value of the payment increases as the deutsche mark depreciates relative to the dollar.

A later section uses these concepts to determine the potential cost of lead/lag decisions.

Long-Term Borrowing and Investment. Long-term investment in foreign countries (especially weak currency countries) raises serious questions concerning sources for borrowing, and concomitantly, a practical way to cover the exposure. The long-term nature of the investment places the hedger in a difficult position. Typically the evaluation of hedging strategies involving borrowing is based on interest costs and forecasted exchange rates. Long-term

TABLE 3.1.   THE EFFECT OF VARYING EXCHANGE RATES ON THE
                    LAGGING PROCESS

Exchange Rate		Dollar Value
($/DM)	(DM/$)	
.38	2.63	97,068
.39	2.56	99,620
.40	2.50	102,178
.4027[a]	2.48	102,873
.41	2.44	104,732
.42	2.38	107,287

[a]Break-even exchange rate.

interest and exchange rate forecasts are generally available through banks for the major countries. However, as forecasts project farther out, their accuracy diminishes. Thus the hedger is provided with little guidance for the long term. Implementing hedging decisions that are based on long-range currency and interest rate forecasts is tantamount to speculation.

Given the currency risk problems related to long-term borrowing, one approach hedgers use to handle the exposure is to allow the invested asset and its financing to work together. Briefly covered in the following sections are two ways that long-term borrowing is used to satisfy debt and/or investment requirements and manage currency risk.

MATCHING.   A technique similar to the local borrowing strategy reviewed earlier involves directly matching the amount and currency denomination of the asset with a liability of the same.[2] Again, this strategy produces direct offsetting of exchange gains and losses. Additionally, a portion of the revenues generated (in SC) by the asset is intended to meet the local borrowing interest expense. Where applicable, the matching concept can result in a safe, conservative hedge.

BORROW WEAK, INVEST STRONG.   This strategy stems from the fundamental asset/liability rule stated earlier in this chapter. That is, hold liabilities in weak currencies and assets in strong ones. Occasionally, firms borrow long term in weak currencies to finance investment in strong currency countries (assuming acceptable interest costs, etc.). Borrowing weak, investing strong does not hedge the exposure, rather it takes advantage of it. The principal aim is to invest in an asset exhibiting the potential to increase or maintain its value, using a liability that is likely to grow less costly in terms of the parent currency. While this approach involves greater currency risk, it does have the potential of producing favorable translation gains over the long run. Alternatively, investment in subsidiaries stationed in weak currency countries occasionally must be financed by parent loans to the subsidiary. In countries where the potential for devaluation is high, using this approach involves considerable risk. Hence the rule is to move the necessary funds in and out as quickly as possible. The subsidiary should consult with local exchange authorities concerning the prepayment of principal and interest, and so forth.

In the following section, parallel loans are introduced as yet another approach to managing long-term exposure. Methods for evaluating alternative strategies and measuring their costs are examined afterwards.

Parallel and Back-to-Back Loans. A parallel or back-to-back loan is a unique lending agreement between firms stationed in different countries. Each company's financial needs must be opposite. Both firms have idle funds denominated in their home currency, and each has a subsidiary in the other's country. Each subsidiary is in need of local (SC) financing. An agreement is made between the companies to exchange a set amount of the desired currencies for a specified time period. The primary difference between parallel and back-to-back loans is that back-to-back loans are negotiated with the right to offset, parallel loans are not. The right to offset means that if one firm should default on all or a portion of its loan, the other firm is permitted to "set off" the amount it is owed against its own loan obligation to the defaulting firm. Parallel and back-to-back loans are especially attractive because they:

1. Represent an alternative source of funds when funding cannot be obtained through traditional modes

2. Can sometimes be negotiated at below-market interest rates, making subsidiary borrowings less costly

3. Effectively erase the foreign exchange risk associated with foreign investment

Consider two multinationals, an American and a German. The U.S. parent has a German subsidiary in need of deutsche mark financing. Likewise, the German company's U.S. subsidiary needs U.S. dollar funds. By negotiating a parallel or back-to-back loan (e.g., a deutsche mark loan from the German parent to the U.S. firm's German subsidiary, reciprocated by a dollar loan from the U.S. parent to the German firm's U.S. subsidiary), all parties benefit. Had subsidiary financing been funded through direct parent investment, both parents would have been faced with potential currency risk problems. Furthermore, independent local borrowing by the subsidiaries could mean substantially higher borrowing costs. Parallel and back-to-back loans make use of otherwise idle cash balances while keeping them in the home country, thereby eliminating foreign exchange risk.

Loans to both parties should have the same maturity and are generally long term (6 to 10 years). Interest rates on the loans are usually fixed according to the commercial rates prevailing in each country. Interest payment terms, the spread between respective interest rates, and security measures are negotiated.

Currency Swaps. As the name implies, a currency swap is merely a currency exchange between two parties. Specifically, it is a spot currency exchange between two companies stationed in different countries, reciprocated by a reverse exchange on some future date. Good swap candidates have similar (but opposite) financing and/or investment needs. For instance, suppose that a U.S. firm with surplus U.S. dollar funds needs British pounds for investment in its British subsidiary. At the same time, a British concern with available pound balances wishes to invest in the United States. The two firms have the following options available to them.

Spot Purchase. Each may purchase the desired foreign currency in the spot market for investment in the foreign country. The cost equals the cost of foregone investment elsewhere. However, opting for this alternative does not solve the foreign exchange risk problems. That is, the foreign investment would not be hedged (or would have to be hedged). Moreover, sometimes country exchange restrictions limit or prohibit the outright purchase of their foreign currency.

BORROW LOCALLY.   Each may choose to invest its idle funds at home while borrowing the desired currency in the local (foreign) marketplace. The cost of doing this is equal to the interest cost differential between lending at home and borrowing abroad. From an accounting perspective, the investment is hedged since the firm is offsetting a foreign currency liability (the foreign currency loan) with a foreign currency asset (the investment).

SWAP CURRENCIES.   Both may agree to mutually swap the desired currencies and reexchange them on a later date, up to 10 years hence. An annual fee reflecting the interest rate differential between the two respective countries is paid by one company to the other. This concept is similar to parallel loans, discussed in an earlier section.

Of the three options outlined, currency swaps often surface as the more attractive alternative. The advantages are similar to those of parallel and back-to-back loans. First, swapping currencies eliminates virtually all foreign exchange risk associated with the respective foreign investments. Second, the interest cost differential negotiated in swap arrangements is frequently more attractive than what could have been achieved if each firm had carried out its financing/investment independently. Third, swap agreements that use idle cash do not affect the firm's debt/equity ratios. Finally, swaps simplify the cumbersome duties associated with arranging hedged, long-term financing and investment.

Choosing Between Debt Alternatives.   Borrowing or lending, in one form or another, is an integral part of many hedging strategies. Earlier sections showed how companies use borrowed funds to finance investment in a subsidiary or support leading or lagging policies. Other methods such as forward contracts (discussed in a later section in this chapter) are indirectly structured around borrowing or lending. It is not unusual to have three or four debt related hedging vehicles from which to choose. If all methods are nearly equal in terms of performance, flexibility, and so on, then the selection of the best hedge is principally a function of cost.

Evaluating potential sources of debt that are denominated in different currencies involves more than simply examining their respective interest costs. Understanding how interest costs are affected by exchange rate changes is critical. Funds borrowed at a high rate of interest may grow less expensive (relative to borrowing at a lower rate) if the exchange rate moves in their favor. Conversely, if caught on the other side of a move, the same borrowing may become overwhelmingly costly. The hedger needs some wherewithall to analyze the current interest rate picture and, based on exchange rate expectations, assess which is potentially the more attractive alternative. One method[3] of comparing borrowing costs and ultimately selecting the optimal borrowing source is described in the following.

Comparing the costs between potential loans is a two-step process. First, the two loans are made comparable by finding the break-even exchange rate required to make them equal in cost. The loans are then evaluated based on the hedger's perception of the future exchange rate outlook. A previous section used the break-even exchange rate (BE_n, Eqs. 3.1 and 3.2) to determine whether to lead or lag deutsche marks. The same principle applies when choosing between alternative sources of debt. Again, interest rates, current exchange rates, and forecasted exchange rates play key roles in the evaluation process. The following equations (Eqs. 3.1 and 3.2) are reprinted for ready reference. As before, a and b refer to the participating countries, i is the interest rate, n is the time in years, and ER_0 represents the current exchange rate.

$$(1 + i_a)^n = [(1 + i_b)^n * ER_0]/BE_n \qquad (3.1)$$

Solving for BE_n,

$$BE_n = [(1 + i_b)^n * ER_0]/(1 + i_a)^n \qquad (3.2)$$

Consider the case of a U.S. manufacturer needing to finance the expansion of its subsidiary in Germany. The firm has the option to either borrow Eurodollars or borrow locally in Germany. Financing is needed for one year; the German borrowing rate is 8 percent (i_a) and Eurodollar rate is 12 percent (i_b). The current exchange rate is DM 1 = $.3600, but the manufacturer expects that the mark will appreciate to $.3800 within the year. The manufacturer would like to determine which source offers the lower borrowing cost.

First, Equation 3.1 is used to find the break-even exchange rate:

$$(1 + .08) = [(1 + .12) * (.3600)]/BE_n$$

Solving for BE_n, using Equation 3.2

$$BE_n = [(1.12) * (.3600)]/(1.08)$$
$$BE_n = \$.3733$$

Assuming interest rates will remain stable over the loan term, the manufacturer can use the BE_n to determine which of the two loans is potentially less costly. In this case, the guidelines for acceptance are:

1. Accept the Eurodollar borrowing if the exchange rate is expected to be greater than the $.3733 break-even point. Any exchange rate below the break-even level would make the Eurodollar loan more expensive relative to the deutsche mark loan.
2. Accept the deutsche mark borrowing if the forecasted rate lies below the break-even point.

Since the manufacturer expects the mark to appreciate to $.3800, the Eurodollar borrowing emerges as the more attractive source. The reasoning behind this decision is best explained as follows: Even though the German interest rate is below the Eurodollar rate (8 percent vs. 12 percent), an appreciating deutsche mark causes deutsche mark interest and principal payments to increase, in U.S. dollar terms.

FURTHER INFORMATION.   Equation 3.1 can be rearranged to produce additional figures useful for comparing the two loans. Solving
Equation 3.1 for i_a reveals the *risk adjusted interest rate* associated
with the Eurodollar loan. This calculation adjusts the Eurodollar
interest rate to reflect the manufacturer's exchange rate forecast.
The forecasted exchange rate is simply inserted into Equation 3.1
in place of the BE_n variable.

$$
\begin{aligned}
i_a &= n[(1 + i_b) * (ER_0)]/BE_n - 1 \quad\quad (3.3)\\
&= [(1.12 * (.3600)]/.3800 - 1 \\
&= 6.1 \text{ percent}
\end{aligned}
$$

By including the exchange rate forecast, the manufacturer's risk
adjusted interest rate becomes 6.1 percent, which is much lower
than the 12 percent Eurodollar coupon. This rate should be used
when evaluating similar borrowing decisions involving the dollar
and the mark. (These same principles apply to estimating the cost
of a lead/lag decision.)

    Conversely, solving Equation 3.1 for i_b calculates the highest Eu-
rodollar rate that the manufacturer would be willing to accept,
given the previously discussed exchange rate conditions.

$$
i_b = n (1 + i_a) / [(ER_0/BE_n) - 1] \quad\quad (3.4)
$$

Or, in the case of the manufacturer:

$$
\begin{aligned}
i_b &= 1 (1.08) /[.3600/.3800 - 1] \\
&= 14.0 \text{ percent}
\end{aligned}
$$

The manufacturer would be willing to accept any Eurodollar rate
up to and including 14 percent. Above 14 percent, the German rate
becomes more attractive.

SUMMARY.   The preceding analyses are not without their problems. First, despite the apparent precision of the equations, the final decision still relies on expectations, or forecasts, of future currency and interest rates. Accurately predicting where these rates
will be in the future has up to this point eluded us. It is ironic that

such forecasts are the building blocks of many of the techniques discussed thus far. Evaluations based on long-term forecasts should include a reasonable margin for error. (In reality, experience tells us that every forecast should include a margin for error.) It is vitally important that a hedge of long duration be reviewed periodically. Second, the equations do not consider tax effects. But despite their shortcomings, these analyses offer a valuable starting point for evaluating debt alternatives.

Estimating Hedge Costs. The true cost of any hedge cannot be known until the exposure period is over and the hedge completed. Yet, understanding the costs prior to implementation is vital to selecting the appropriate technique. Regrettably, at the outset these costs can only be estimated: If we knew them there would be no reason to hedge at all!

Asset and liability adjustment hedges generally deal with the borrowing of funds in one currency and the investments of the same in another. The cost of these types of hedges is the net of the two transactions adjusted for taxes and estimated currency risk. The estimated cost is a function of five factors: real interest rates, taxation, time, present exchange rates, and forecasted exchange rates. Equations 3.5 and 3.6 are used to find the potential cost. Equation 3.5 finds net i_a, the after-tax, risk-adjusted cost/return of borrowing or investing in the exposed currency. Equation 3.6 finds the same, but for the currency that is not exposed. Note that a and b refer to the participating countries, i is the interest rate, ER_0 is the spot exchange rate, and ER_n is the exchange rate forecasted to prevail at time n.

$$\text{Net } i_a = [(1 + i_a)^n * (ER_n/ER_0) - 1] * (1 - \text{tax rate})_a \quad (3.5)$$

$$\text{Net } i_b = [(1 + i_b)^n 1] * (\text{tax rate})_b \quad (3.6)$$

A Case. A U.S. manufacturer has a three-month DM 250,000 intercompany payable to its German subsidiary. The manufacturer suspects the deutsche mark will rise, is considering leading payment, and would like to know the potential cost. Interest rates are 6.0 percent in Germany (country a) and 11.5 percent in the United

States (country *b*). The U.S. tax rate is 50 percent, the rate in Germany is 40 percent. The current exchange rate is DM 1 = $.36; the rate forecasted three months out (*n* = .25) is $.37. The manufacturer's leading process can be summarized as follows:

1. Borrow the U.S. dollar equivalent of the deutsche mark payable at the 11.5 percent U.S. rate

2. Exchange the borrowed dollars for deutsche marks at the spot price

3. Lead payment (prepay the deutsche mark payable) to the subsidiary

4. Invest the deutsche marks for three months at the subsidiary level, earning 6 percent (or put to equally profitable use)

ESTIMATING THE COST. The net estimated cost of leading payment to the subsidiary is simply the interest cost of borrowing the U.S. funds less the interest revenue received from investing the prepayment in Germany. Because the transactions take place between two countries, special attention must be given to the different tax structures and forecasted exchange rates. This procedure is outlined in Steps 1 through 3.

Step 1 Find the after-tax cost of the U.S. borrowing (net i_b):

$$\text{net } i_b = [((1 + .115)^{.25} - 1) * .50] \qquad (4.6)$$
$$\text{net } i_{US} = 1.38 \text{ percent}$$

Step 2 Find the after-tax, risk adjusted interest rate earned on the deutsche mark investment (net i_a):

$$\text{net } i_a = [((1 + .06)^{.25} - 1) * (.37/.36)] * (1 - .40) \qquad (3.5)$$
$$\text{net } i_{DM} = 0.905 \text{ percent}$$

Step 3 Net Steps 1 and 2:

$$\text{net} = (1) - (2)$$
$$= 1.38 - .905$$
$$\text{net} = .475 \text{ percent}$$

TABLE 3.2.   ESTIMATING THE COSTS OF LEADING PAYMENT

	US dollars
Dollar loan:	
DM 250,000 * $.36/DM	90,000
Interest expense (3 months, after-tax):	
$90,000 * [(1.115 − 1) * 0.5]	(1,241)
Interest earned on DM 250,000:	
DM 250,000 * (1.06 − 1) = DM 3,668	
Adjusted for exchange rate forecast:	
DM 3,668 * $.37/DM = $1,357	
After-tax:	
$1,357 * 0.6	814
Payment of principal	(90,000)
Net estimated cost	(427)

Note: "*" indicates multiplication.

Subtracting the interest earned (.905%) from the borrowing cost (1.38%) gives the net estimated cost of leading payment. Thus the potential cost incurred by leading payment to the subsidiary is $427, i.e. (90,000, * .00475). Table 3.2 illustrates the prepayment in dollar terms.

The estimated cost can be compared with the cost of other strategies that hedge the same exposure.

Pricing Policies

Building the hedge directly into everyday foreign exchange transactions is yet another effective way to minimize the potential exposure. Pricing policies are price manipulative strategies designed to create, wherever possible, hedges within the product sales price. Such policies are activated automatically and continuously by the firm's daily operations. Thus the obvious advantage of these hedges is their reliability. Their effectiveness, however, is influenced by the hedger's ability to accurately anticipate long-term exchange rate trends and the product market's willingness to accept sales price changes.

Sales Price and Invoice Adjustments. Businesses that transact in countries whose currencies are expected to devalue often adjust product sales prices to reduce foreign currency risk. For example, suppose that a U.S. manufacturer has a German subsidiary that has traditionally invoiced in deutsche marks. Forecasts predict that the mark will weaken 5 percent against the U.S. dollar over the coming three months. While sales denominated in devalued marks will not produce losses at the subsidiary level, their translated dollar value will generate foreign exchange losses at home (see Chapter 2). Given the anticipated deutsche mark weakening, the manufacturer may consider instructing the subsidiary to raise deutsche mark denominated sales prices proportionately. It may not be possible to raise the price, since sales price increases may be met by a lag in sales volume, especially since a local currency devaluation may not immediately affect other local manufacturers' pricing structures.

Invoice adjustments are another alternative. If a longer term depreciation of the currency of billing is expected, rather than merely adjusting sales prices, management may consider changing the invoice currency altogether. For instance, West German firms that perceived in the early 1980s a long-term weakening of the mark relative to the U.S. dollar would have found the decision to invoice in dollars a rewarding one. By 1984, the value of the deutsche mark had fallen more than 45 percent. The initial costs of invoice adjustments are typically associated with modifying the present systems to account for changes in the currency of billing. Sales volume may not be significantly affected since sales prices converted at the spot rate will not show any immediate change, other than the fact that the product will be priced in the converted currency. Longer term costs will hinge on the accuracy of management's foresight, of course. In order to maintain operating, accounting, and marketing consistency, frequently changing the currency of billing is not recommended. Thus this strategy should only be considered when management perceives a long-term currency trend. Moreover, in the case of a currency that has already moved considerably, one can never be certain that the trend will continue (the techniques of Part 2 address the trend question).

Transfer Pricing. Multinationals that operate subsidiaries in weak currency or underdeveloped countries can encounter problems when they attempt to repatriate earnings from the subsidiary to the parent. Weak currency countries commonly utilize exchange controls that restrict the outflow of capital from their economies (see Chapter 5). Obviously, this is a concern to multinationals, since assets held in depreciating currencies create losses when valued in the parent currency.

Transfer pricing is not so much a hedging strategy as it is a cash management tool. Specifically, transfer pricing is the incremental raising and lowering of intercompany selling prices to facilitate the transfer of income between operating units. In the case of transferring funds out of restricted countries, this technique can help to achieve two common goals: (1) transferring income from weak currency countries to strong ones; and (2) moving pre-tax income out of a country with high tax rates and into one where the income will be taxed at a lower rate.

Consider the manufacturer who, due to foreign exchange controls, has been unsuccessful in remitting earnings from its subsidiary stationed in an underdeveloped country. If the manufacturer conducts a large number of transactions with the subsidiary, it might consider placing artificially high prices on sales to the subsidiary, while simultaneously paying slightly lower prices on purchases from it. As a consequence, the subsidiary's income is reduced due to higher intercompany operating costs and lower sales revenue. The foregone income is transferred to the parent in the form of greater intercompany sales revenue and lower operating costs. This same concept may be used to move income into countries where it will be taxed at a more favorable rate.

Transfer pricing policies require an intensive, centralized function to oversee intercompany flows, and are particularly effective for businesses with high intercompany traffic. But, it should be strongly noted that foreign exchange and tax authorities are keenly aware of such activities and take measures to prevent them. Transfer pricing programs must, therefore, be implemented on a continuing basis using only marginal price differentials.

Foreign Currency Accounts

Businesses that commonly execute transactions (both incoming and outgoing) in foreign countries often establish foreign currency accounts with banks in those countries (some countries prohibit such accounts). A foreign currency account is a foreign exchange deposit held at a local bank to facilitate the handling of many foreign exchange transactions. Rather than converting each transaction into the home currency, the transactions are accounted for as they pass through the foreign currency account. Here, offsetting foreign currency receivables and payables are grouped and matched against each other. Grouping receipts and payments not only reduces administrative and transaction costs, but in many cases eliminates the need for hedging altogether.

Although foreign currency accounts are, for the most part, a cash management tool, their balances do represent foreign currency assets, and consequently, potential exposures. Thus these accounts can act as a hedge against company liabilities in the same currency. But when they do not offset similar liabilities, they become exposures themselves.

Cross Hedging

Cross hedging is the offsetting of exposures in two (or more) currencies. Cross hedges are, of course, only successful when the two currencies behave similarly. A prime example of two *sister* currencies is the Dutch guilder and the West German mark. A study over the 1980–1985 period shows a correlation coefficient of .935 (1.0 is perfect) between the two currencies; Chapter 9 shows a .984 correlation between the British pound and the Australian dollar. One might expect to find similar relationships between the U.S. and the Canadian dollar, many of the European Economic Community (EEC) currencies, and so forth.

A potential cross hedger might be a manufacturer with Dutch guilder receivables and deutsche mark payables of nearly equal duration and amount. The firm might choose to let the two exposures *cross-offset* each other, rather than hedging each individually. Here, the manufacturer is anticipating that the mark and the guilder will move in tandem, if they move at all. If the currency values decline, the manufacturer loses on the less valuable guilder receivables but gains on the less costly deutsche mark payables. The opposite applies to a joint appreciation of the two currencies. In both cases, the manufacturer achieves near equal offset at virtually no hedge cost.

The preceding scenario is a model example. The value of the deutsche mark could have increased while the guilder declined. If this were true, the manufacturer would have actually doubled its losses rather than neutralizing them. Or, the guilder could have fallen much more sharply than the mark. Losses on the guilder receivables would greatly outpace any gains on the deutsche mark receivables. Thus cross hedging involves a considerable degree of speculation since the hedger, essentially, will always be holding two or more open positions. Moreover, one can never be assured that currencies that have correlated strongly in the past will do so in the future. Some divergence between currency values should always be expected and included in the anticipated cost of the hedge.

An alternative to cross hedging two individual currencies is to hedge using a *basket* approach. The International Monetary Market (IMM) in Chicago and the Financial Exchange (FINEX) in New York (both are futures exchanges) have developed two new futures contracts that may be suitable for cross hedging, particularly in the less liquid currencies. The IMM offers a futures contract based on the European Currency Unit (ECU), while the FINEX trades the U.S. Dollar Index. Both are based on a basket of 10 currencies. A description of the ECU and the U.S. Dollar Index, along with contract specifications, can be found in Appendix 4. Futures contracts will be discussed later in this chapter. As of June 1986, these new instruments are still in their infancy. Trading volume in both contracts is still too light to support any type of hedging program.

Cross hedging is more of a basic strategy than it is a specific technique. It is most practical (although not strongly recommended) for those businesses that commonly have offsetting exposures in highly correlating currencies. Even so, cross strategies are perhaps most often used when the firm is unable to construct a hedge using the exposed currency. This problem often arises among businesses with transactions in less common or restricted currencies (these are often the same). In such cases, a correlation study between related currencies may uncover a suitable hedging partner. The hedger can then borrow, lend, or use any number of external methods to cross-protect the exposure.

EXTERNAL TECHNIQUES

Complementing the internal hedging methods, there are also a wide variety of hedging instruments and strategies obtainable from outside the firm. The first, most basic, and most widely used of such techniques is the forward contract. A forward contract is an agreement between two parties to buy or sell a currency at a stated price on some future date. Forward types of agreements (in rudimentary form) have been negotiated between merchants for probably as long as history has been recorded. Early examples have been found in ancient Greece and Rome.[4] Likewise, forward foreign exchange contracts have been negotiated since money first became a recognized commodity. Today, the broad acceptance of the interbank forward contract has spawned a growing selection of external hedging measures designed to meet the varied needs of international companies. Among these are foreign exchange futures and currency options. The forward foreign exchange contract and its derivatives are detailed in the following sections.

Chapters 1 and 2 were careful to recognize the importance of measuring exposure from an after-tax perspective. Likewise, it is critical that exposure be *managed* on an after-tax basis as well. Not only does taxation influence the value of the hedge, but the tax consequences of hedging from within foreign nations may exclude some techniques from the hedging process altogether. Tax considerations may be, therefore, crucial to both the initial evaluation of a potential strategy and the calculation of the amount necessary to fully protect the exposure.

The tax considerations associated with the external hedging methods are not included in the following sections, but are instead reserved for Chapter 4. Similar provisions apply to most methods, and their application is relatively straightforward once the technique is fully understood. The examples used in Chapter 3 are reproduced in Chapter 4 and modified to reflect the effects of taxation.

[Forward Foreign Exchange Contracts

A forward foreign exchange contract is an agreement between a bank and a bank customer to exchange one currency for another on a future date. The exchange rate, delivery date, and amount of the contract are all fixed at the time of the agreement. Forward contracts are principally designed to offset the hedger's perceived currency risk. Thus their use as a vehicle to ensure earnings and cash flow has increased as the currency markets have grown more volatile. A typical forward hedger could be a U.S. manufacturer who has just purchased some equipment from a vendor in London. The purchase is negotiated in British pounds, due in 90 days. If in the interim the pound appreciates relative to the dollar, the manufacturer loses because the dollar value of the British payables has increased. At the same time the purchase is negotiated, however, the manufacturer also contracts with its banker to buy the pounds 90 days later at a specified exchange rate. In doing so, the manufacturer effectively *locks in* the future value of the British pound payables and eliminates its currency risk. Any loss on the payables is offset by an equal gain on the forward purchase. Herein lies the attractiveness of the forward contract. Forward contracts allow the hedger to determine and establish the value of future cash flows. Costs can then be managed and sales prices set so that a reasonable margin for profit can be achieved.

Forward foreign exchange contracts are virtually identical to borrowing or lending the same amount of foreign currency for the duration of the exposure period. A forward purchase is equivalent to lending the foreign currency. Similarly, a forward sale mirrors the act of borrowing the currency over the same time frame. Thus forward deals are closely related to the borrowing/lending techniques discussed earlier, the main difference being that the banker has entered the picture and greatly simplified the process for the hedger.

FORWARD RATE QUOTING. If the quoted forward rate of a currency is more expensive in U.S. dollar terms than the spot rate, the currency is said to be at a premium. Conversely, if the quoted rate is lower than the spot rate the currency is at a discount. As in any typical buy/sell situation, the aim is to *buy low, sell high.* Thus, implicit in the hedger's quoted forward rate is the bank dealer's bid/ask spread. The bank covers its transaction costs and makes its profits through the spread. For instance, if the dealer is willing to sell pounds six months forward at $1.4465, he or she would no doubt offer to buy them for only, say, $1.4455. (The same applies to the futures and options markets covered in later sections of this chapter, except that the spread is created on the exchange floor instead of at the dealer's desk.) The spreads are reasonably small for the actively traded currencies. Note, however, that the spread grows considerably wider in less liquid markets. The point to be learned here is not that your banker or broker is a thief, but that the bid/ask spread within the forward premium or discount is a direct cash flow out of the market. In a standard forward (or futures) contract hedge, where the hedge is usually a one-time event, the bid/ask spread represents a loss to the hedger that cannot be recouped.

Consider the same U.S. firm of the preceding example. On March 16, 1984 the manufacturer agrees to purchase the equipment from the London vender for BP 1 million. Payment is to be in pounds on delivery of the equipment, estimated to be six months hence (September 17, 1984). Over the coming six months, if the value of the pound rises relative to the dollar, the firm will be forced to pay more (in dollar terms) when it purchases pounds to remit payment. The U.S. firm decides to offset this risk by purchasing BP 1 million six months forward. On March 16 the spot exchange rate is BP 1 = $1.4465 and pounds six months forward are quoted at 1.4603.[5] Since the forward rate is greater than the spot rate this forward contract is at a premium. That is, whereas today (March 16) the firm could pay $1,446,500 for the pounds, in six months the bank is willing to sell the same pounds for $1,460,300. The premium on the pounds is $13,800. In equation form, where FR_c is the contracted forward rate and SR_0 is the spot rate at the inception of the forward contract, the premium or discount on a forward contract is:

$$(FR_c - SR_0) * \text{contract amount} \qquad (3.7)$$

Or, in the case of the British pound forward purchase:

$$(1.4603 - 1.4465) * \$1,000,000$$
$$= \$13,800$$

FORWARD CONTRACT COSTS AND COVERAGE. The cost of forward hedging is commonly assumed to be the premium or discount on the contract. (This is not entirely correct, and we address this misconception later.) In the case of the U.S. manufacturer, the estimated cost of the equipment is $1,460,300: $1,446,500 plus the $13,800 forward contract *insurance* payment. Assuming that this is a real world example (the rates are actual), let us proceed to the end of the exposure period and evaluate the final results.

TABLE 3.3.   FORWARD CONTRACT HEDGE TRANSACTIONS

		Dollar Value
	Forward Contract Hedge	
March 16:	1. Agree to purchase equipment costing 1,000,000 pounds. Spot rate = 1.4465	($1,446,500)
	Negotiate forward contract. Forward rate = 1.4603.	
	2. Premium = (1.4603 − 1.4465) * BP1,000,000	(13,800)
	3. Estimated equipment cost; (1) + (2)	($1,460,300)
September 17:	Equipment delivery; purchase BP from banker at agreed forward rate.	
	4. Final equipment cost = (1.4603 * BP1,000,000)	($1,460,300)
	5. Change from estimated cost; (3) − (4)	0

Note: "*" indicates multiplication.

The equipment is delivered on September 17. The forward contract expires and the manufacturer purchases BP 1 million from his banker for the agreed $1,460,000 price. Table 3.3 outlines the transactions that took place over the life of the hedge.

Given that the pound has fallen from 1.4465 to 1.2335, Table 3.4 combines the forward hedge and the exposure to show the offsetting effects.

The forward purchase offsets the exposure as planned, the only difference being the cost of the premium. Tables 3.3 and 3.4 are good illustrations of the most attractive feature of a forward contract hedge; namely, it guarantees a price.

However, the forward contract does have its drawbacks. Table 3.4 shows that if the manufacturer had not hedged, but instead waited to purchase the pounds spot on delivery of the equipment, $213,000 would have been saved over the projected cost. This translates to a savings of $226,800 over the cost of the forward contract. If the manufacturer could have saved $213,000 by not hedging, then what is the real cost of the forward contract hedge?

There are two schools of thought regarding the calculation of the cost of forward contract hedging. The most common, as previously described, assumes that the cost is simply the forward premium paid or received. Two factors, one based on ignorance and the other on theory, probably account for this widespread belief. First, the forward rate is often the only *future* exchange rate known at the inception of the hedge. This leads many hedgers to use the forward rate as a forecast, and therefore, to believe erroneously that this

TABLE 3.4. OFFSETTING EFFECT OF A FORWARD CONTRACT

		Forward Purchase	Exposure
March 16:	1. Estimated equipment cost; Spot rate = 1.4465 Forward rate = 1.4603	($1,460,300)	($1,446,500)
September 17:	2. Actual cost	$1,233,500	($1,233,500)
	3. Change from actual; (1) + (2)	($226,800)	$213,000
Difference:			$13,800

gives an accurate measure of the cost. Second, the findings of academic research on the relationship between spot and forward rates[6] support the theory that the forward rate is an unbiased predictor of the future spot rate. In other words, over the long run the mean value of the deviations between the future spot rate and the forward rate (plus transaction costs) has been found to be very close to zero. Thus assuming efficient markets[7] and ignoring transaction costs, the estimated cost of hedging in the forward market should be equal to the cost of remaining unhedged.[8] Over the long run this theory may, in fact, be true. But this fact does not imply that an individual forward rate is a good predictor of the future spot rate. On the contrary, the quoted forward rate merely reflects the difference between the interest rates prevailing in the two respective countries (ignoring transaction costs, expectations, etc.). (Previous sections in this chapter discussed the interest rate/foreign exchange rate relationship in detail.) The forward rate is neither intended nor designed to forecast exchange rates. Thus, the real cost of a forward contract should not be limited to the premium or discount.

The second school of thought assumes that in addition to the premiums or discount, the gain or loss on the exposure that would have been realized had the firm remained unhedged should also be considered. This value, of course, cannot be known at the inception of the hedge. Equation 3.8, where FR_c is the contracted forward rate and SR_b is the spot rate on settlement of the contract, accounts for the unhedged potential gains and losses and can be used to determine the true cost of a forward contract hedge.

$$\text{Actual cost} = (FR_c - SR_b) * \text{Amount of contract} \qquad (3.8)$$

(The hedger can estimate true cost by inserting a forecasted spot rate in place of SR_b.)

Referring back to the equipment example and using Equation 3.8, the actual cost of the forward contract hedge (including the forward contract premium) is:

$$\text{Actual cost} = (1.4603 - 1.2335) * \text{BP } 1,000,000$$
$$= \$226,800$$

Equation 3.8 calculates the actual cost of the forward contract hedge at $226,800, or about 16 percent of the total value of the equipment. Although this value may appear very large, remember that the market could have easily gone the other way. If the pound had appreciated the same amount, the forward contract could have saved the manufacturer about $200,000.

PUTTING IT ALL INTO PERSPECTIVE

We have illustrated two methods used to establish the cost of a forward contract hedge. The first, where the cost is assumed to be the discount or premium, only applies to the very long term and to the most efficient markets. The second, where gains and losses on the unhedged position are included, is certainly more practical on a transaction-by-transaction basis. This approach, however, is not without its gray areas too. In the case of the U.S. manufacturer, we would be incorrect to argue that the true cost of the previously discussed forward contract hedge amounted to the full $226,800. There is considerable value in the elimination of risk, but assigning a dollar figure to it can be a difficult task. In the end, establishing the true cost of the hedge should be a melding of both approaches. Since the real value of the forward contract lies in its ability to eliminate the hedger's currency risk, each firm should analyze its hedging objectives and determine the level of risk it is willing to assume. Is *no risk* worth $226,800 or a fraction thereof? Moreover, the hedger must acknowledge the fact that on commitment to a standard forward contract hedge the firm is exposed to another form of risk: the risk of forgoing exchange gains on the unhedged exposure. If the hedger has the ability to discern probable exchange rate trends beyond the point of random guessing (Part 2 shows that this can be accomplished), then these potential gains do have considerable value and should be included in the measurement process.

Interest Rate Parity.   As banks and corporations engage in forward foreign currency deals, foreign exchange must be borrowed and lent. The forward rate of a currency is equal to its present value plus the interest to be earned on assets denominated in that currency over a stated time period. Accordingly, the interest rate differential between two countries' currencies (based on Euromarket rates) will be reflected in their foreign exchange rates. This concept, known as interest rate parity (IRP), is probably best understood through an example.

Suppose a U.S. bank customer wishes to purchase British pounds 90 days forward. Before the bank promises to oblige, it must first know how much it will cost to be assured of having the pounds on hand in 90 days. In order to do so, the bank effectively does the following:

Day 1: 1. Borrow the U.S. dollar equivalent at the U.S. 90-day Euromarket rate
        2. Convert the borrowed dollars into British pounds at the spot exchange rate
        3. Invest (lend) the pounds at the British 90-day Euromarket rate

Day 90: 1. Deliver the pounds to the customer for U.S. dollars

If the U.S. dollar borrowing rate differs from the British lending rate, the bank will gain or lose by an amount equal to the Euromarket rate differential. The bank, therefore, will sell the British pounds forward at either a premium or a discount. In general, the currency of the country with the higher interest rate will trade at a forward discount to the currency of the country with the lower interest rate. Conversely, the currency of the country with the lower interest rate will trade at a forward premium to the currency of the country with the higher interest rate.

A simple formula can be used to determine the forward rate implied by the interest rate differential. In equation form:

$$FC_n = FC_{spot} \left[(1 + i_{US}{}^n) / (1 + i_{FC}{}^n) \right] \tag{3.9}$$

Note that FC_n is the implied forward rate, FC_{spot} represents the spot exchange rate, n equals the number of years (for a 90-day period, $n = .25$), and i represents the prevailing Euromarket rate for the respective time period. Thus the three-month ($n = .25$) implied forward exchange rate for a spot rate of $1.3980 and three-month Euromarket rates of .09750 and .09375 for the U.S. dollar and British pound are respectively:

$$FC_{(.25)} = 1.3980 \left[(1 + .0975)^{.25} / (1 + .09375)^{.25} \right]$$
$$FC_{(.25)} = 1.3992$$

We find the implied rate, $1.3992, very close to the actual (1.3996). Table 3.5 shows the implied forward rates compared to the actual quoted rates over various time periods.

Notice that the implied and quoted forward rates are consistently close; however, as the time period increases the gap between the implied and the quoted rate often widens. This is generally done to protect the bank from unforeseen risks.

The forward contract discussion stated that forward rates are not intended to predict future exchange rates. Rather, by quoting forward rates based on their interest expenses, banks effectively hedge the forward contracts they negotiate with their corporate customers. The example just discussed helps to show that this is true.

Option-Date Forward Contracts. Option-date forwards are designed for the hedger who has an exposure but is unsure of its duration. Whereas with standard forward contracts the settlement date is fixed, option-date forwards allow the hedger the *option* to settle at any time between two specified dates. Thus these contracts add a measure of flexibility otherwise unattainable through a standard forward contract. The option-date delivery period may be contracted between spot and some future date, or between two future dates, for example, between five and six months from spot. Since

TABLE 3.5.   IMPLIED VS. QUOTED FORWARD RATES FOR THE
BRITISH POUND (1/24/84)

Time Period	British Pound Euromarket Rate	Dollar Euromarket Rate	Spot Rate	Implied Forward Rate	Quoted Forward Rate
Spot			1.3980		
1 month	.091875	.095625		1.39840	1.39850
3 months	.093750	.097500		1.39920	1.39960
6 months	.095625	.099375		1.40039	1.40110
12 months	.098750	.103125		1.40357	1.40530

option-date forwards allow the hedger to settle virtually anytime between the two dates, when quoting option-date rates the bank always assumes that the customer will settle the contract at the worst time (for the bank). The customer, therefore, receives the least attractive rate, that is, the highest premium or the lowest discount quoted for the option-date time period.

Suppose a U.S. manufacturer knows that it will need to purchase British pounds sometime between spot (June 1) and December 1. The manufacturer wishes to be hedged over the entire period, since it may require the funds today, in three months, or even six months from now. Therefore, the firm negotiates an option-date contract allowing for settlement anytime between June and December. On June 1 the spot and forward buying rates are as follows:

Spot	$1.5400
November 1 (forward)	$1.5200
December 1 (forward)	$1.5150

The bank would offer to sell the pounds forward at the 1.5400 spot rate. In quoting the higher rate, the bank protects itself from the possibility that the manufacturer may purchase the pounds immediately. (Had the bank quoted the lower December rate (1.5150) and the firm asked for settlement immediately, the bank would have been forced to sell the pounds at a loss.)

Forward Forward Contracts.   A forward forward contract is a forward contract negotiated from one future date to another. Available in the major, more liquid markets, these contracts offer the hedger greater flexibility (relative to standard forwards) at, oftentimes, lower cost.

Forward forwards are most often used by hedgers that are aware of their future transactions, as in the case of this U.S. manufacturer. On March 16, 1984 the manufacturer knows that on June 15 it will purchase a piece of British equipment. The price tag is BP 1 million and payment is due three months after purchase (September 17). Thus the total time period extends for six months—from March 16, when the firm knew of its future purchase, through the September

17 payment date. But the manufacturer is only exposed over the second half of the period, from June 15 to September 17. If management expects the pound to appreciate over the initial three months, they would probably hedge immediately to take advantage of a perceived good forward buy on pounds. Alternatively, if a future pound decline is foreseen, waiting until the purchase is finalized (three months) to negotiate the forward purchase may prove less costly. In this case, assume that the manufacturer does expect the pound to appreciate over the near term and wants to hedge immediately. There are two ways that the manufacturer can use the forward market to place the hedge:

1. Negotiate a standard forward contract covering the entire six-month period. As in the previous section, the firm buys pounds six months forward to be assured of a hedge. The initial cost of this approach is equal to the cost of the six-month forward premium.

2. Arrange a forward forward contract covering the latter three months. This is done by buying the pounds six months forward and simultaneously selling pounds three months forward. Here, the two contracts offset each other over the initial three months but create a forward purchase hedge over the remaining period. The cost is equal to the difference between the premium paid for the six-month forward purchase and the premium received from the three-month forward sale.

Table 3.6 shows that the initial cost of the two approaches differs only in the amount of premium paid or received. On March 16 the spot exchange rate is BP 1 = \$1.4465, the three-month forward rate is \$1.4528, and the six-month forward is \$1.4603.

The forward forward contract hedges the three-month exposure period for nearly half the premium cost of the standard.

Futures Contracts

Futures contracts are yet another outgrowth of forward type agreements and the need to establish *future* prices to facilitate planning in the present. It follows then that the basic elements of a futures

TABLE 3.6. COMPARISON BETWEEN PREMIUM COSTS OF
STANDARD AND FORWARD FORWARD CONTRACTS

Standard forward:	= 6 month forward rate − spot rate
	= (1.4603 − 1.4465) * 1,000,000
	= $13,800
Forward forward:	= 6 month forward − 3 month forward
	= (1.4603 − 1.4528) * 1,000,000
	= $7,500

Note: "*" indicates multiplication.

contract mirror those of the forward type examined in the previous
section. Both consist of an agreement between two parties to exchange a good or service at some future time for a specified price.
The main difference is that forward contracts are generally tailored
to the hedger's individual needs; futures contracts are standardized. Another difference that is often important is that forwards
are generally for a fixed term, while futures can be disposed of or
added to on any market day.

The modern futures markets developed out of a basic need for
free and competitive trading of the world's primary commodities:
grains, meats, and metals. Four leading features are necessary to
achieve this end: (1) free entry and exit for all participants, (2) a
commodity that is standardized in quality and quantity, (3) an active marketplace with many traders, and (4) continuous availability
of complete, inexpensive, and easily accessible information.[9] Today, futures contracts are offered in many categories other than just
grains, meats, and metals. There are futures on petroleums, interest rates of many varieties, stock and commodity indexes, and of
course, foreign exchange. With few exceptions, all contain the necessary requirements of free and competitive trading.

Foreign Exchange Futures

BACKGROUND. Foreign exchange futures were introduced in
1975 by the International Monetary Market (IMM) division of the
Chicago Mercantile Exchange. To facilitate free, uninterrupted

trading, currency futures contracts are standardized and available only in the most broadly traded world currencies; namely, the British pound, deutsche mark, Swiss franc, Japanese yen, and Canadian dollar. The French franc, Dutch guilder, Italian lire, Mexican peso, European Currency Unit and the U.S. Dollar Index are also offered but see limited actual trading. Contracts are arranged for delivery on the third Wednesday of March, June, September, and December. Like forward contracts, futures can be settled by accepting or making delivery of the specified currency on expiration of the contract. But most of the time (95 percent), futures contracts are settled by reentering the market with an offsetting purchase or sale of an equivalent contract(s) before the expiration of the contract.

Bank forward contracts usually do not require a cash deposit to hold the position (but they may deplete credit lines). Futures contracts must be backed by a margin (or earmarked money) deposit. The minimum margin requirement is generally equal to about 5 percent of the contracts' dollar value. Over the life of the position this amount may fluctuate as the value of the contract changes. For instance, if the futures position began to show a loss equal to, say, one half the margin requirement, the hedger may be issued a *margin call* for additional margin money in order to hold the position. Funds placed on margin are a direct cost of futures hedging, and probably a key reason why currency futures are not used as broadly as they could be. A less well-known fact is that frequently up to 100 percent of the hedger's margin deposit may be placed in an interest bearing account earning the current U.S. treasury bill or money market rate. Thus the real margin cost is not the full cost of capital that the hedger could otherwise have earned on the margined funds, but rather the difference between the hedger's cost of capital and the interest earned on the margin account. Futures are akin to other exchange traded items (stocks, etc.) in that the transaction cost associated with assuming a position is the broker's commission. In forwards the banker's *commission* is implicit in the bid/ask spread.

The dollar value of currency futures contracts presently (1986) varies around $50,000. Thus 20 or more futures contracts may be necessary to establish a $1 million equivalent hedge (see Appendix 4 for futures contract specifications). The quoting of futures is similar to that of forwards. That is, the rate quoted for a given currency future is directly related to the interest differential between the foreign currency and the U.S. dollar. As a consequence, the quoted rate of a currency future with three months to expiration is equivalent to the rate quoted on a three-month forward contract in the same currency. When this is not the case, arbitragers are eager to take advantage of the risk-free windfall created by a divergence in the two rates. Any disparities are quickly brought back into alignment.

CURRENCY FUTURES AS A HEDGING TOOL. Futures operate identically to forwards with respect to the initial placement of the hedge. Consider again the manufacturer with six-month payables totaling BP 1 million. On March 16, the manufacturer buys British pound futures contracts to protect itself from a potential appreciation in the pound. Like the standard forward, the underlying intent of the futures hedge is to offset any gain or loss on the exposure with a corresponding loss or gain on the futures position.

On March 16, British pounds six months forward were quoted at $1.4603. The September 1984 future was priced at $1.4590 (closing price), very close to the forward. As each futures contract is equal to BP 25,000 (Appendix 4), the manufacturer purchases 40 futures contracts to hedge the BP 1 million exposure (40 * 25,000 = 1,000,000). Commission fees are assumed to be $100 per contract. Table 3.7 illustrates the futures hedge and its approximate cost and compares these figures with those of the forward contract and no hedge scenarios detailed in Tables 3.3 and 3.4.

Table 3.7 shows that the final equipment cost (7) under the futures hedge is $7,500 less than its estimate (3). The forward, on the other hand, showed no change in its estimate. Although the future emerges cheaper in this case, the opposite may prove true another time. The minor fluctuation in the futures cost relative to a similar forward stems from what is termed futures *basis risk*, and is due largely to the method of delivery. Most forward contracts are settled by physical delivery of the currency at the previously agreed rate. Conversely, less than 5 percent of futures contracts result in physical delivery. Instead, they are settled via reentering the marketplace with an offsetting trade. The actual currency needed to

TABLE 3.7. ITEMIZED FUTURES CONTRACT HEDGE COSTS AND A
COMPARISON TO THE COSTS OF A SIMILAR FORWARD HEDGE

		Dollar Value
	Futures Contract Hedge	
March 16:	Agree to purchase equipment valued at BP 1,000,000. Spot rate = 1.4465.	
	1. Purchase 40 futures contracts. Future rate = 1.4590. (40 * BP 25,000 = BP 1,000,000)	
	Futures cost = BP 1,000,000 * 1.4590	(1,459,000)
	2. Commission = 40 contracts @ $100 ea.	(4,000)
	3. Estimated equipment cost; (1) + (2)	(1,463,000)
September 17:	Equipment delivery; close out futures contracts via offsetting trades. September futures rate = 1.2410	
	4. Loss on futures position = (1.4590 − 1.2410) BP 1,000,000 * .2180	(218,000)
	5. Purchase pounds in spot market. Spot rate = 1.2335	(1,233,500)
	6. Add in commission fees [from (3)]	(4,000)
	7. Net equipment cost; (4) + (5) + (6)	(1,455,500)
	8. Change from estimated cost; (7) − (3)	$7,500
	Forward Contract Hedge (from Table 3.3)	
	9. Estimated equipment cost	(1,460,300)
	10. Net equipment cost	(1,460,300)
	11. Change from estimated cost; (10) − (9)	$0
	Forward vs. Futures	
	Net equipment cost (futures)	1,455,500
	Net equipment cost (forward)	1,460,300
	Difference	$4,800
	No Hedge (from Table 3.4)	
	12. Estimated equipment cost	(1,446,500)
	13. Net equipment cost	(1,233,500)
	14. Change from estimated cost; (12) − (13)	$213,000

Note: "*" indicates multiplication.

complete the transaction is then acquired through the cash market. Thus it is critical that the futures market correlate closely with the cash. And the two do behave very similarly, but the synergy is not perfect. The figures of Table 3.7 can be used to illustrate the concept of basis change. On March 16, the spot rate is 1.4465 while the future is 1.4590. By September 17, the spot rate has dropped to 1.2335, for a net decline of .2130. Likewise, the future has fallen by .2180 to 1.2410. In other words, a one point drop in the spot British pound was accompanied by a 1.02 point decline in the future. The change in the future relative to the cash was very close, but it was not exact.

THE HEDGE RATIO. The futures/cash relationship can be used to refine the futures hedge to offset the cash exposure more correctly. One way is to divide the change in the spot price by the change in the future[10] thus determining the *hedge ratio* for a pair of instruments. In this case, the hedge ratio is the number of futures contracts required to perfectly offset a one point move in the underlying spot price.

$$\text{Hedge ratio} = \frac{\text{Change in spot price}}{\text{Change in future price}}$$

$$= \frac{.2130}{.2180}$$

$$= .97$$

The manufacturer would have actually needed less than 40 futures contracts to fully hedge the exposure. Specifically, a BP 1 million hedge would require:

$$.97 \times \frac{\text{BP } 1,000,000}{\text{BP } 25,000/\text{contract}}$$

or, 38.8 contracts.

For large exposures, the hedge ratio should be monitored often and the hedge adjusted accordingly. A more detailed discussion of this topic is presented in the next section.

A second point brought forth by Table 3.7 is the fact that the manufacturer could have saved $213,000 by remaining unhedged. Recall that the standard forward contract hedge of the previous section produced similar results. Both hedges protected the exposure, but neither recognized the potential for windfall gains. This will always be true for any hedge that is placed immediately and held for the duration of the exposure. Futures contracts are more flexible in this area. Their standardization permits a more active role in exposure management.

FUTURES CONTRACT SETTLEMENT FLEXIBILITY.   The ability to enter and exit a hedge at any time is a valuable option, given the fluctuations witnessed in today's floating currency markets. We noted earlier that futures contracts differ from forwards in that they are generally settled through an offsetting purchase or sale prior to the expiration of the contract, not by actual delivery. Since a futures hedge may be withdrawn, replaced, and so on at any time, it would seem that futures contracts offer the hedger a powerful exposure management tool, albeit at a somewhat greater risk.

Is it possible for the manufacturer, using the power of free entry and exit, to minimize the *opportunity costs* associated with classical forward and futures hedging? We believe so. Recall that in previous examples, immediate, permanent placement of a standard forward or futures hedge (Figures 3.5 and 3.6) resulted in lost opportunity costs of $226,800 and $213,000, respectively. We have devoted most of Part 2 to demonstrating how these opportunities can be captured.

The Hedge Ratio.   We noted in the previous section that if a future is used for the hedge there may not be an exact correspondence between the hedge and the actual cash. In this section we study the hedge ratio in greater detail. Gay and Kolb, writing in the *Journal of Portfolio Management* developed several approaches to the measurement of how many futures are needed for a given cash exposure.[11] Gay and Kolb's work covered interest rate futures, but earlier, Hill and Schneeweis[12] addressed the problem for currencies. A simple derivation of the hedge ratio appeared recently[13] and we will follow that study here. First we let:

$$P = S + nF \tag{3.11}$$

where P = Value of a portfolio
        S = Spot or actuals in the portfolio (the exposure)
        F = Futures in the portfolio
        n = Number of futures

Now we want the change in P to be zero with any change in the spot and futures prices. This is required by the hedge. Therefore:

$$DP = DS + nDF \tag{3.12}$$

or,

$$0 = DS + nDF \tag{3.13}$$

where D is an operator, roughly signifying differentiation or difference. Solving for the number of futures, n:

$$n = -DS/DF \tag{3.14}$$

In words, the hedge ratio, n, is the negative of the change in the price of the actuals divided by the change in the future price. This value can be found from the data. The monthly values for the British pound over the year 1983 are shown in Table 3.8.

While there was some month-to-month fluctuation, the British pound hedge ratio stayed very close to one, on balance. For the year, the ratio was not significantly different from unity. For the present there is no problem with covering exposure in British pounds with futures of the same dollar amount.

Foreign Currency Options

Currency options are a new kid on the foreign exchange block—the black sheep, the runt of the litter. Yet the black sheep sometimes yields the finest wool and the runt of the litter often grows to be the most beautiful. Currency options have taken a giant step toward filling a significant void in today's foreign exchange marketplace.

TABLE 3.8.   HEDGE RATIO VALUES FOR THE BRITISH POUND
OVER 1983

Month	DF	DS	n
January	−4.56	−4.04	−0.88
February	−4.26	−4.51	−1.06
March	−3.70	−4.12	−1.11
April	5.37	4.89	−0.91
May	3.37	3.27	−0.97
June	−2.22	−2.39	−1.08
July	−1.73	−2.11	−1.22
August	−2.56	−2.38	−0.93
September	−0.68	−0.48	−0.71
October	0.01	−0.09	9.00
November	−2.03	−1.94	−0.96
December	−4.29	−4.43	−1.03
Total	−17.28	−18.33	−1.06

But they are far from being understood, accepted, and used to their fullest advantage.

This section introduces foreign currency options with examples to aid the potential hedger. We point out that option premiums are like insurance premiums with the important difference that the option buyer may get back considerably more than he or she pays. We review the recently introduced currency options traded on the Philadelphia Stock Exchange (PHLX) and the International Monetary Market (IMM). Using the exchange-traded options as a cornerstone, we examine the key ingredients that distinguish options from forward and futures contracts, why these factors are important to the hedger, and how and when hedgers can use options to their advantage. Finally, we present the major uses of currency options for commercial hedging purposes and illustrate the four principal option strategies for the hedger.

We begin with a section briefly discussing option fundamentals, valuation, and the usefulness of profit graphs in understanding option strategies.

Option Fundamentals.   Before discussing the uses of currency options in hedging foreign exchange, it may be helpful to become familiar with commodity options in general. To begin with, options are of two types: *calls* and *puts*. A call is the right, but not the obligation, to buy the underlying future at a specified price within a specified time period (a long hedger is a call buyer). A put is the right, but not the obligation, to sell the underlying future for a specified price within a specified time period (a short hedger is a put buyer). The specified price at which the option holder has the right to buy or sell is known as the *exercise price*. In exchange for the right to buy or sell, the option buyer pays the option seller (writer) a quoted price, or *premium*.

Option premiums reflect price expectations. An investor anticipating a price rise would buy a call or sell a put. Conversely, an investor expecting price decline would sell a call or buy a put. Positions may be closed out in a variety of ways. For the option holder (buyer), if the underlying market price moves against the option, the holder merely allows the option to expire. Conversely, if the underlying market price moves in favor of the option and the option becomes profitable, the holder may either exercise the option (*call* the seller) or sell the option to another buyer in the marketplace. In the case of the option writer, if the price moves against the option, the writer will eventually be *called*, that is, requested to make good on his or her promise to sell at the specified exercise price (the writer may of course buy the option back at a loss prior to being called). If the underlying market price moves in favor of the option the writer does nothing and retains the premium.

RISK AND RETURN.   Unlike futures positions, where both risk ✳ and return are potentially unlimited, the option holder has potentially unlimited return while bearing only limited risk. Losses on option purchases are limited to the amount of the premium paid. The option writer's risk/return picture is a mirror image of the option holder's. That is, return is limited to the amount of the premium while risk is potentially unlimited. Consequently, writing options are generally considered speculative and rarely recommended for hedging. Table 3.9 summarizes the option fundamentals.

✳ VALUATION.   The option premium represents the market's perception of the option's true value. The premium is composed of

TABLE 3.9.   OPTION MARKET FUNDAMENTALS

	Type of Market	Risk	Method of Close Out
Call holder (Long call)	Rising	Limited to premium paid	Expiration, exercise, or sell out
Call writer (Short call)	Declining, flat	Potentially unlimited	Be "called," retain premium or buy back
Put holder (Long put)	Declining	Limited to premium paid	Expiration, exercise, or sell out
Put writer (Short put)	Rising flat	Potentially unlimited	Be "called," retain premium, or buy back

two parts: *intrinsic* value and *time* (extrinsic) value. Intrinsic value is the immediate profit to be made from exercising an option. A call option has intrinsic value anytime the underlying market price exceeds the exercise price. A put has intrinsic value (IV) when the market price is below the exercise price.

$$\text{Calls: IV} = \text{Underlying Market} - \text{Exercise} \qquad (3.15)$$
$$\text{Price (MP)} \qquad \text{Price (XP)}$$

$$\text{Puts: IV} = \text{Exercise} - \text{Underlying Market} \qquad (3.16)$$
$$\text{Price (XP)} \qquad \text{Price (MP)}$$

Options having intrinsic value are commonly referred to as being *in-the-money*. *Out-of-the-money* options have no intrinsic value. A long call, for instance, is out-of-the-money when the spot market price is below the exercise price. Both puts and calls are said to be *at-the-money* if the underlying market price equals the exercise price.

Often, options are priced greater than their intrinsic value. The difference between the option's premium and its intrinsic value is the option's time value (TV).

$$\text{TV} = \text{Option premium} - \text{Intrinsic value} \qquad (3.17)$$

The time value of an option represents the probability that the option will become profitable or increase in value. Time value is influenced by several factors: (1) the underlying spot price, (2) the option's exercise price, (3) time remaining until the option expires, (4) underlying market volatility, and (5) short-term interest rates. Let us expand on the latter three points; time, volatility, and short-term interest rates. First, the greater the time remaining until expiration the higher the probability that the option will turn profitable. But time is a wasting asset. As time decreases, the time value of the option gradually diminishes until it reaches zero on the date of expiration. At this point, the only value remaining (if any) is the option's intrinsic value. Second, volatility is a measure of the amount by which the commodity or currency has fluctuated over a given time frame. Some markets operate relatively smoothly with little fluctuation while others fluctuate wildly. One form of volatility is commonly expressed as the standard deviation of percentage of market returns. The larger the standard deviation the greater the probability that an option will turn profitable or increase in value. Finally, when an investor places cash up front in options rather than in an alternative instrument such as treasury bills, the investor incurs opportunity cost associated with the option investment. Because the investor could otherwise be earning interest on the treasuries, the option premium should be discounted to reflect the foregone interest return. As the interest rate rises the value of the premium falls. The short-term interest rate, or the risk-free rate of interest, is the rate generally used in the valuation of commodity options. Figure 3.1, where XP is the exercise price and MP represents the underlying market price, shows the relationship between the intrinsic and time value of a call option.

Notice that time value is greatest when the call is at-the-money ($MP = XP$). As the option moves further into the money the time value diminishes as the intrinsic value grows. The intrinsic/time value relationship of a put is a mirror image of Figure 3.1.

PUTTING THE FUNDAMENTALS INTO PERSPECTIVE. An actual numerical example will clarify the principles. Data for the British pound trading on the PHLX over the two-week period of June 6 through June 17, 1983 are used for the illustrations.[14] Using Equations 3.10 and 3.12, Table 3.10 shows the relationship between intrinsic value, time value, in-the-money, and out-of-the-money for a September 1983 call on British pounds at various exercise prices. The

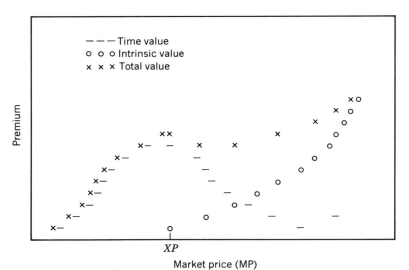

Figure 3.1. The relationship between the intrinsic and time value of a call option.

average spot exchange rate over the period was $1.5517. The option quotation units are U.S. cents per British pound (see Appendix 3 for option specifications). Remember that the option's time value is greatest when the call is at-the-money (the 155 exercise price is very near the 1.5517 spot rate). Note also that the 145 and 150 calls each show negative time values. Deep in-the-money calls, as is the case with the 145 call, are often priced lower than their intrinsic value. Less expensive calls (at-the-money) tend to return greater percentage profits, given an equivalent exchange rate change.

TABLE 3.10. INTRINSIC/TIME VALUE RELATIONSHIPS AT
VARIOUS EXERCISE PRICES FOR THE SEPTEMBER 1983
CALL ON BRITISH POUNDS

XP	Premium	Intrinsic Value	Time Value	In-the-Money	Out-of-the-Money
145	8.60	10.17	− 1.57	X	
150	5.00	5.17	− 0.17	X	
155	1.80	—	1.63	X	
160	0.50	—	0.50		X
165	0.20	—	0.20		X

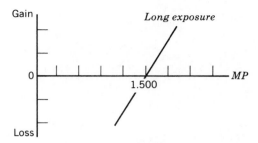

Figure 3.2. Long exposure.

USING PROFIT GRAPHS. Conceptualizing the effects of holding forward futures and options, or options in combination with forwards/futures, and/or the underlying exposure, is often confusing. Profit graphs allow the hedger to easily see the potential effects of holding such positions. Moreover, they are additive. Combining profit graphs for different positions not only shows the result of holding individual positions, but also shows where the total position risk lies. Profit graphs are particularly useful for illustrating option positions and strategies. They permit the investor to see quickly the potential effect on a position given a change in the underlying market price.

The examples that follow will almost always be accompanied by a profit graph. Figures 3.2 through 3.4 show the profits for long and short exposures and the classical forward/futures contract hedge. These are the two fundamental hedging positions that have been discussed up to this point. In a later section the profit pictures of a long call and a long put are explained. In all cases, dashed lines represent individual positions and solid lines show the net position achieved by combining all positions in the strategy. Gains or losses are shown on the vertical axis while the underlying market price, quoted in dollars per foreign currency, is plotted horizontally.

LONG EXPOSURE; RECEIVABLES IN FOREIGN CURRENCY. Suppose a U.S. manufacturer has three-month British pound receivables and the spot exchange rate is $1.500. Figure 3.2 shows that if the pound appreciates the firm gains on the exposure (dashed line). Conversely, the receivables lose value if the pound falls. Also shown is

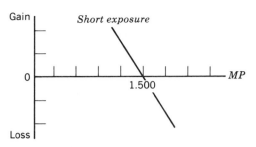

Figure 3.3. Short exposure.

the extent of the manufacturer's risk. By allowing the receivables to remain exposed the firm faces potentially unlimited losses. Theoretically, should the pound fall to zero the manufacturer would lose the entire exposure.

SHORT EXPOSURE; PAYABLES IN FOREIGN CURRENCY. Now assume that the U.S. manufacturer has exposed British pound payables. The gain/loss picture is a mirror image of the long receivable position (see Figure 3.3).

LONG EXPOSURE, SHORT FORWARD/FUTURES HEDGE. As noted in the previous sections, the classical external approach to hedging foreign currency receivables or payables is to assume an opposite position in the forward or futures market. Figure 3.4 depicts the effects of hedging exposed payables (S) by purchasing the exposed currency in the forward or futures market (L).

Gains and losses on the exposure (S) are almost perfectly offset

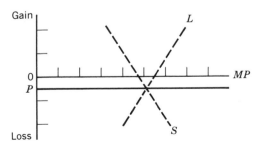

Figure 3.4. Long exposure, short hedge.

by losses or gains on the hedge (L). The final result appears as a bold horizontal line located in the loss region. In the case just discussed the negative net value represents the forward or futures premium paid. Pounds bought in the future at a discount would have created a bold horizontal line in the *gain* region.

Options and Hedging. For the currency hedger, options possess three distinct qualities unattainable through alternative hedging methods such as futures or forwards. By purchasing an option contract the hedger: (1) limits foreign exchange risk to the price of the premium, (2) retains the potential to profit on the exposure, and (3) increases risk management flexibility.[15]

LIMITED RISK AND RETAINED PROFIT POTENTIAL. Standard futures/forward hedges protect exposed positions from both unfavorable and favorable rate changes; there is no avenue for gain. In fact, futures and forward commissions and bid/ask spreads virtually guarantee a loss (see the previous section). Options also provide the offsetting feature that is critical to a successful hedge. But unlike forwards or futures, options permit the hedger to capitalize on favorable exchange rate moves.

A case in point: A U.S. manufacturer has three-month payables denominated in British pounds. The spot exchange rate is BP 1 = $1.5000. If the pound appreciates in the interim, the firm will incur a loss as the British payables grow more expensive in dollar terms. Conversely, a depreciating pound causes the payables to become less costly. The manufacturer hedges by purchasing a 150 call option on British pounds, in other words, the right to buy pounds at $1.5000. The manufacturer pays $.03 premium for the option. Three months later the pound has risen to 1.6000, and the firm exercises its option to buy pounds at 1.5000. This translates to a net protection of $.07 (.10 savings less the .03 premium expense). For the price of the premium, the option has protected the firm by significantly offsetting the spot market loss.

Now, consider the reverse situation: Over the three-month period the pound has declined to 1.4000. The British payables are less expensive (in dollar terms). In this situation, the firm chooses to ignore its option. The manufacturer gains $.10 on the exposure

(1.5000 − 1.4000) and forgoes the $.03 premium expense for a net gain of $.07. At all times the firm's risk is limited to the premium expense, it cannot lose more. Meanwhile, the option still allows for possible foreign exchange gains.

How does the option differ from the common forward/futures hedge? Consider the example previously discussed. Assume that instead of purchasing an option, the firm buys pounds forward through its bank. Assume also that pounds are selling at a forward premium equal to the option premium.[16] If the exchange rate rises to 1.6000, the futures/forward hedge protects the manufacturer in the same manner as the option purchase. But what if the pounds decline to 1.4000? Even though pounds have become cheaper in the spot market, the manufacturer is locked into buying them at the 1.5300 forward rate. Consequently, the manufacturer experiences a $.13 loss on the forward/futures purchase.

RISK MANAGEMENT FLEXIBILITY. Known limited risk and the power to exercise anytime or simply allow the option to expire, permits the hedger using options to manage currency risk more accurately in a number of special situations. One such situation is a firm bidding on a construction project in a foreign country. If the proposal is denominated in the foreign currency, surely the firm would like to protect the currency flows involved. Unfortunately, the bidding firm is uncertain whether the bid will be accepted. Prior to the inception of currency options, hedging contingent currency flows through the forward or futures markets sometimes proved extremely costly. In the event that the bid was not accepted, the rejected bidder was left carrying a forward or futures position, possibly at a loss. Bank negotiated options were rare and generally too expensive to justify their use. Now, exchange traded currency options (more banks are writing options, too) help ensure that contingent flows are reasonably protected. In addition, the hedger is not burdened by an open exposure if they do not materialize (see the section entitled "Hedging contingent currency flows" for a more detailed discussion).

Option Positions for Hedging Purposes. Much of today's option talk centers around an ever changing mix of intricate trading strategies.

A simple long call or put rarely seems to enter the conversation. But when the potential risk is known, corporations generally hedge (externally) by assuming an opposite position in the currency markets. When applied to options, this translates into buying a call or put. Innovative schemes like spreads, straddles, or strips do not apply. Moreover, because writing options is considered speculative and the tax laws treat it as such, short calls and puts are not recommended for hedging. The process of elimination brings us back to the two main strategies used in hedging with currency options: the long call and long put. The mechanics of these two positions will now be summarized.

THE LONG CALL. The option hedger wishing to protect an exposure from an increase in the value of the exposed currency would buy a call(s). Figure 3.5 shows the profit graph for a call purchased for premium (p). The call holder pays the premium for the right to buy the currency at the agreed exercise price (XP).

As long as the underlying exchange rate (MP) remains below the exercise price, the call holder would not exercise the option since the currency can be bought cheaper in the spot (or futures) market. In fact, the call holder probably would not exercise until the underlying exchange rate exceeds the exercise price by at least the amount of the premium. The point on Figure 3.5 where the profit line (dashed) crosses the horizontal axis is the option holder's break-even point (A). Any exchange rate increase beyond the break-even intersection signifies a gain on the option position. Note also that the lower portion of the dashed line is horizontal

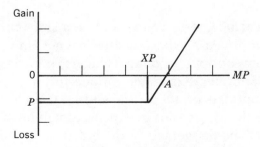

Figure 3.5. Long call.

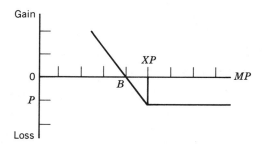

Figure 3.6. Long put.

(and negative). This indicates that regardless of the extent of the potential exchange rate drop, the call holder is never at risk for more than the premium paid.

THE LONG PUT. The option buyer wishing to protect against a decline in the value of the exposed currency would buy a put(s). A long put is illustrated in Figure 3.6.

A comparison of Figures 3.5 and 3.6 shows that a long put is simply the mirror image of a long call. Thus as long as the underlying exchange rate remains above the exercise price, the put holder probably would not exercise the option (the currency may be sold at a higher rate in the spot futures market). Accordingly, the put holder probably would not exercise until the underlying exchange rate has moved through the break-even point (B). Any exchange rate decline beyond the break-even point produces a gain on the option position. The option premium, or in this case the extent of the hedger's risk, is again represented by the negative portion of the horizontal dashed line.

Commercial Hedging Uses. Who should consider currency options as a hedging tool? And what are the major commercial hedging uses of currency options to date? Hedgers, both large and small, should include foreign exchange options in their hedging collection. Option contracts on the PHLX and IMM are small enough to appeal to firms desiring to hedge exposures valued at under $1 million (remember, banks generally do not deal for less than that). Those hedging on a grander scale and/or in the less actively traded currencies may turn to their banker. As will be pointed out in a later section, major commercial banks are beginning to offer options on a somewhat limited basis.

We have already mentioned that hedgers buy calls to guard against price increases and buy puts to offset potential price declines. Classical forward or futures type hedges shield the exposure from any exchange rate change (up or down). Options, on the contrary, give the hedger the opportunity to reap some of the benefits of a favorable exchange rate move while continuing to protect the exposure. These qualities lend options particularly useful to hedging contingent exposures. But options can also be used to hedge receivables, payables, foreign investments, and the like. The examples that follow illustrate how.

Table 3.11 contains the PHLX option data that are used for each example. Here, XP and MP are the exercise and underlying market price, respectively. Option premiums are quoted in cents per British pound. For instance, the out-of-the-money Sep83 call at 155 is priced at 1.80 cents, or $225 per contract of BP 12,500 (see Appendix 3 for option specifications). Note that we use premiums quoted over a two-week period. Thus some discrepancy between premiums for puts and calls does exist.

HEDGING ACCOUNTS RECEIVABLE: LONG PUT. On June 17, 1983, our U.S. manufacturer has three-month receivables totaling BP 100,000. The spot rate is 1.5517 (see Table 3.11, period 1). To guard against future exchange rate declines the manufacturer purchases eight Sep83 British pounds puts exercisable at 1.5500. The premium expense is 5.2 cents per contract, or $5,200 for all eight.

$$\text{Premium} = .052 * 12,500 \text{ pounds}$$

or, $650 per contract.

$$\text{Total premium} = (8 \text{ contracts}) * \$650$$
$$= \$5,200$$

Figure 3.7 displays the profit picture of the BP 100,000 receivable hedged with September 1983 155 puts.

TABLE 3.11.   BRITISH POUND OPTION DATA TRADING ON THE
PHLX OVER VARIOUS PERIODS IN 1983

Period 1: 6/6-6/17   *Spot price (average): 1.5517*

XP	Calls			Puts		
	Sep83	Dec83	Mar84	Sep83	Dec83	Mar84
145	8.60	14.00	—	1.00	—	—
150	5.00	7.00	—	2.50	2.90	—
155	1.80	4.60	—	5.20	—	—
160	.50	3.00	4.40	—	—	—
165	.20	1.40	—	—	—	—
Future:	1.5515	1.5527	1.5541			

Period 2: 8/22-9/2   *Spot price (average): 1.5076*

XP	Calls			Puts		
	Sep83	Dec83	Mar84	Sep83	Dec83	Mar84
145	8.00	5.60	8.90	.10	1.05	1.85
150	.70	2.80	5.85	1.10	2.95	2.40
155	.10	.75	2.20	4.80	6.00	—
Future:	1.5069	1.5087	1.5106			

Note: A two-week period is required due to the lack of suitable daily liquidity in the PHLX market at this time. Options on futures trading on the IMM in Chicago have since been introduced. From their inception these contracts have traded at significantly higher volume levels than their PHLX cousins.

Judging by the net position line (bold), if the pound falls below 1.5517 the manufacturer's total risk exceeds the cost of the option premium ($5,200). This occurs because the options are hedging an exposure contracted when the spot exchange rate was lying above the exercise price. Unless the exposure is contracted when the underlying market price equals the exercise price, the exchange rate risk related to the exposure must be included. In this case the exercise price is 1.5500 and the spot price is 1.5517. Therefore, the manufacturer assumes $170 of additional risk related to the exposure. The hedger's total position risk is $5,370. Moving up and to

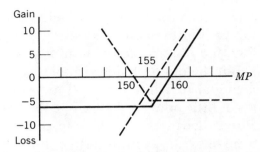

Figure 3.7. Hedging receivables with a long put.

the right along the net position line, note that any pound rise above 1.6037 produces an overall gain on the hedge.

Suppose now that September arrives and the U.S. manufacturer collects the British receivables. Because the pound has depreciated 4.41 cents to 1.5076 the manufacturer liquidates its option to sell pounds at 1.5500. The eight 155 puts are sold for their intrinsic value, or 4.80 premium price (see Table 3.11, period 2). Table 3.12 outlines the hedge transactions and the final outcome.

The cost of the option hedge equals the gain or loss on the exposure plus the gain or loss on the hedge, or $6,210. At greater than 5

TABLE 3.12. EXPOSED RECEIVABLES HEDGED WITH A LONG PUT

		Dollar Value
June 17:	1. BP 100,000 exposed receivables Spot rate: = 1.5517, estimated value	155,170
	2. Purchase 8 Sep83 155 Puts; Premium = 5.2 cents	(5,200)
September 2:	Receive BP receivables; close out option hedge via offsetting put sale	
	3. Premium received = 4.4 cents	4,400
	4. Net premium expense; (3) + (2)	(1,800)
	5. Sell BP 100,000 spot @ 1.5076	(150,760)
	6. Loss on exposure; (5) + (1)	(4,410)
	7. Net receipts; (6) + (4) + (1)	148,960
	8. Net loss on receivables; (7) − (1)	(6,210)

percent of the total exposure value, this hedge does not appear particularly attractive. Furthermore, the option does not fare well when contrasted with a classical forward/futures hedge under the same conditions. But the option holder is not paying just for protection, but is paying also for the potential to profit on the exposure. Over periods of little or no exchange rate fluctuation the classical forward/futures hedge will often out-perform the option hedge. Of course, no one truly knows ahead of time that the market will be flat over the exposure period. If the uncertainty is low enough, the hedge is usually unnecessary.

HEDGING ACCOUNTS PAYABLE: LONG CALL. This example operates under the same conditions as the previous one but this time the manufacturer uses call options to hedge payables totaling BP 100,000. As before, the exposure is contracted on June 17 when the spot exchange rate is \$1.5517. To guard against a potential exchange rate increase the firm purchases eight Sep83 155 calls for a premium of 1.8 cents, or \$1,800 in all.

$$\text{Premium} = .018 * \text{BP } 100,000$$
$$= \$1,800$$

Figure 3.8 shows the profit chart of the BP 100,000 payables hedged with Sep83 155 calls.

Even though the option risk is limited to the \$1,800 premium expense, the net position risk is actually less (\$1,630; see bold line).

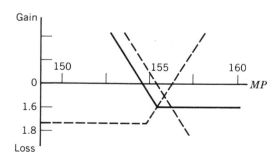

Figure 3.8. Payables hedged with a long call.

Again, this occurs because the spot rate (1.5517) at the time of the option purchase is above the 155 exercise price.

It is now September and the manufacturer remits the BP 100,000 payment. As before, the spot rate has fallen 4.41 cents to 1.5076. Since the market price is below the exercise price the manufacturer could allow the option to expire; however, according to Period 2 in Table 3.11 the 155 calls still have .10 cent remaining in time value. Thus the manufacturer exits the option hedge via an offsetting call sale. Table 3.13 outlines this hedge transaction and the final outcome.

In the final analysis, using British pound call options to hedge the British payables over the above exposure period would have generated a $2,710 gain on the manufacturer's total position.

HEDGING CONTINGENT CURRENCY FLOWS. The hedging task becomes uniquely difficult in cases where the hedger does not have a confirmed exposure, but rather an exposure that may or may not surface in the future. The classical example of a potential exposure of this sort is the industrial firm whose project bid is denominated in a foreign currency. Once the bid has been submitted, the awarding party usually has an allotted time period for bid evaluation. Not

TABLE 3.13. EXPOSED PAYABLES HEDGED WITH A LONG CALL

		Dollar Value
June 17:	1. BP 100,000 exposed payables Spot rate: = 1.5517, estimated value	(155,170)
	2. Purchase 8 Sep83 155 Calls; Premium = 4.8 cents	(1,800)
September 2:	Remit payment; close out hedge via offsetting call sale	
	3. Premium received = .1 cents	100
	4. Net premium expense; (3) + (2)	(1,700)
	5. Buy BP 100,000 spot @ 1.5076	(150,760)
	6. Gain on exposure; (5) − (1)	4,410
	7. Net cost of payables; (4) + (5)	(152,460)
	8. Net gain on position; (7) − (1)	2,710

only is there no guarantee that the firm's bid will be accepted, but the very exchange rates that the bid was based on are free to move.

For example, suppose a U.S. manufacturer has submitted a BP 1 million bid on a project in London. If the bid is accepted the firm will receive an initial payment of BP 500,000 to begin work. The manufacturer encounters one major obstacle: receipt of the BP 500,000 is contingent on being awarded the contract, and notification is three months away. A depreciating pound over the evaluation period could easily diminish the manufacturer's profit margin, or even produce a loss on the project. Prior to submitting the bid the firm has several alternatives by which to attempt to cover its contingent risk:

1. Do nothing
2. Inflate the project bid as a buffer against potential exchange rate fluctuation
3. Sell British pounds forward or sell futures contracts
4. Purchase British pound put options

Unless the firm's policy dictates no hedging, or management is convinced that there will be no adverse exchange rate moves, the first alternative would probably be considered too risky. The second alternative, inflating the project bid, makes the bid less competitive. Raising the project price too much increases the probability that the bid will not be accepted at all. Third, selling pounds forward or selling futures contracts will hedge an exposure, but the exposure exists only if the project is awarded. In the event that the bid is rejected the forward/futures contract becomes a short exposure that must be liquidated (possibly at a loss) or hedged itself. Finally, buying British pound options not only protects the contingent exposure from a pound depreciation exchange, but also limits the manufacturer's risk to the premium cost if the bid is rejected. Thus if the pound appreciates, the puts expire unexercised (or are sold for any remaining time value). Moreover, the manufacturer profits by any pound decline in excess of the premium expense.

HEDGING FOREIGN INVESTMENTS. Those who invest abroad or those abroad who invest in the United States realize the impact fluctuating exchange rates can have on the net return on a foreign investment. The return will improve or deteriorate depending on which direction the exchange rate has moved over the investment period. Buying puts and calls can help to ensure the investor that his or her return will be preserved while still permitting improved return if the exchange rate moves in favor of the investment (but the cost of the options does reduce the expected return).

For example, consider an investor who, in September, has idle funds to invest for three months. The investor buys 1,000 shares of common stock in a British company at BP 50 per share. Since the spot exchange rate is BP 1 = $1.5000, the BP 50,000 investment is worth $75,000. Any appreciation of the pound over the investment period would improve return on the investment (when expressed in dollars). Conversely, a devalued pound could diminish or possibly erase the return entirely. To hedge the return, the investor purchases four December 150 puts at a 2.95 cent premium per option. The investor's total premium expense is $1,475 (Table 3.11, Period 2). Hedging the investment with reasonably priced put options can help to establish a base return while still permitting improved return if the pound appreciates significantly.

By December the British stock is valued at BP 60/share, up BP 10 from September. The investor sells the investment for a BP 10,000 profit. Table 3.14 compares the effects of various exchange rates on the net return (in dollar terms) of the investment hedged with options, with the same investment that is not hedged.

Table 3.14 shows that buying puts to hedge foreign investment has a smoothing effect on the investor's return. As the pound appreciates the hedged return decreases relative to the unhedged (due to the option premium expense). Conversely, as the pound depreciates the hedged return increases, since gains on the option positions partially offset foreign exchange losses tied to the investment. The smoothing effect is shown graphically in Figure 3.9.

By investing in foreign securities, the investor has the potential to benefit through: (1) appreciation and/or earnings of the security and (2) appreciation in the currency of denomination. However, currency fluctuation is a well-known two-edged sword. While currency appreciation will enhance the investor's return, depreciation may erase it entirely. Currency options can reduce the variability of foreign investment return caused by fluctuating exchange rates.

TABLE 3.14   HEDGING FOREIGN INVESTMENT WITH PUT OPTIONS

	No Hedge	Hedged with Four December 150 Puts
September: Spot = $1.5000		
$ Value	75,000	75,000
Option value	0	1,475
Total	75,000	76,475
December: Spot = $1.6000		
$ Value	96,000	96,000
Option value	0	0
Total	96,000	96,000
% Return	+28%	+25.5%
December: Spot = $1.4000		
$ Value	84,000	84,000
Option value	0	5,000
Total	84,000	89,000
% Return	+12%	+16.4%

Hedge Costs and Risk Coverage.   Because the option holder never actually has a genuine commitment to buy or sell the underlying currency, hedging with long puts and calls requires no margin deposit (or subsequent margin calls). The up front premium expense is all that is ever needed to hold the option position. The same does not apply to other option strategies such as writing, spreading, and so on.

Premium costs are determined by the spot price, available strike prices, and the level of risk the hedger is willing to tolerate. An at-the-money option, where the exercise price is equal to the underlying market exchange rate, will usually have a premium greater than the equivalent futures contract basis. (Futures basis, the futures rate minus the spot rate, is similar to the premium or discount on a forward contract.) The option's time value and built-in profit potential are credited for the premium/basis disparity. As exercise prices move out-of-the-money, the premium decreases. Thus one can reduce up front hedge costs by purchasing cheaper, out-of-the-money options. However, this strategy creates a sort of exchange rate gap that may result in inadequate coverage if a major currency

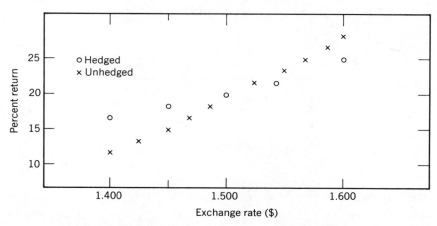

Figure 3.9. Smoothing effect on net return created by hedging foreign investment with put options.

move develops. Near-the-money options will more accurately protect the exposure. In the following discussion, we compare the costs of a standard long forward/futures hedge with the cost of call option hedges placed at various exercise prices. The example suggests that cheaper, out-of-the-money options embody potentially far greater currency risk than near-the-money or forward/futures options.

In January 1984 the spot exchange rate is DM 1 = $.3563. A U.S. manufacturer has deutsche mark payables that are due in March. The manufacturer runs a hedge cost analysis between long forward/ futures and option hedges to determine which to use. Table 3.15

TABLE 3.15. COST COMPARISON: MARCH DEUTSCHE MARK CALI VS. MARCH FUTURES/FORWARD HEDGE (1-19-84)

Futures Forward			Option			
ER Spot	ER March	Basis	XP	March Premium	Intrinsic Value	Option Cost
.3563	.3593	.0030	35	1.06	.063	.0043
			36	0.45	0	.0045
			37	0.20	0	.0020
			38	0.09	0	.0009

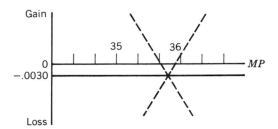

Figure 3.10. Profit graph of the futures/forward hedge.

compares the futures/forward basis cost against the option premium expense (less any intrinsic value) at various exercise prices. Commissions are not considered since they would cost nearly the same for all instruments.

The near-the-money March 36 call is more expensive than the futures basis. As the exercise price moves out of the money the option cost declines to a point where the 37 and 38 calls become cheaper than the futures. Now examine the profit graphs in Figures 3.10 to 3.12.

Figure 3.10 shows that by using the forward or futures contracts the hedger is never at risk for more than the $.003 premium (bold line).

However, note also that the classical futures/forward hedge allows no opportunity for gain. Gains and losses on the exposure are offset by an equal, opposite loss or gain on the futures/forward position. The hedger's risk is covered at an expense equal to the net position line (solid line showing a loss) shown on the graph.

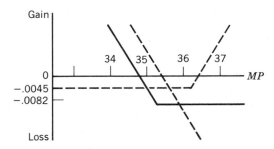

Figure 3.11. Profit graph of the near-the-money call hedge.

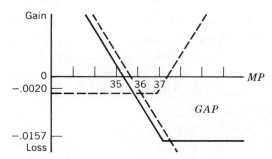

Figure 3.12. Profit graph of the out-of-the-money call hedge.

The profit chart for the near-the-money 36 call, Figure 3.11, indicates that the hedger's risk on the option position is slightly greater at $.0045. Total risk, however, is closer to .0082. Notice that if the mark falls below .3457, the manufacturer still gains on the total position.

Figure 3.12 illustrates the same deutsche mark exposure, this time hedged with an out-of-the-money 37 call.

This option hedge only begins to cover the hedger's risk once the deutsche mark appreciates above .3700. Thus a significant gap develops between the spot rate (.3563) and the call exercise price (.3700). Within the gap, the out-of-the-money call hedger risks to lose much more than the futures/forward premium (even though the option's initial costs are less). Beyond .3720 the option begins to cover the exposure and no further losses occur. Notice that this hedge still allows the hedger to profit from rate moves below .3543. By reducing up front costs this hedger has substantially increased his or her risk.

Bank-Negotiated Options. Prior to the initiation of currency options on the PHLX, and later on the IMM, banks had been writing options only on a limited basis and to the best of their corporate clients. With the new option interest generated by the exchanges, banks are now writing options with greater frequency.

Unlike exchange options, bank over-the-counter (OTC) options are not standardized. Banks write options on many currencies other than those traded on exchanges, at any exercise price, and for time periods ranging from one day to several years out. As far as costs are concerned, smaller contracts seem to be cheaper on the PHLX, but as the contract size approaches $20 million, bank option deals become less expensive than exchange-traded ones.[17] The OTC options also are offered in a variety of ways. Whereas most exchange options are of the American type (exercisable at any time prior to the expiration date), banks offer both American and European style options (European options are exercisable only on the expiration date). In addition, some banks offer fixed exercise price options (similar to exchange options), limited options where the customer agrees to exercise but the premium is deferred until the expiration date, and options on options.[18] The OTC option fundamentals and risk/reward characteristics are virtually identical to those already covered by previous sections.

Synthetic Forward Contracts

Banks are not the only source for forward contracts. Clearly, forward dealing through one's banker is easier and often the most cost effective route. But, there may be times when a forward contract is not available through traditional modes. Perhaps the amount is too small or the firm does not have access to forward deals, and the like.

The recipe for forwards, like Grandma's special cookies, can be written down on the back of an envelope and followed at home. In a sense, forwards can be *synthesized* with the aid of a few guidelines. As noted in a previous section, forward foreign exchange rates are based on the interest rate differential between the two respective countries. Thus borrowing/lending the exposed foreign currency and simultaneously lending/borrowing the funds in the home currency enables the hedger to imitate the standard forward contract hedge. Like the standard, synthetic forward contracts are of two basic forms: (1) the synthetic forward sale and (2) the synthetic forward purchase.

The following two examples illustrate synthetic forward contracts designed to protect exposures in British pounds. In addition to hedging the exposure, note that the interest paid or received on the foreign borrowing/lending is also exposed and should be hedged. In this case, British pound futures contracts are used to

TABLE 3.16.   EXCHANGE AND INTEREST RATES USED IN
EXAMPLES (6/30/82–12/30/82)

Date	Currency	Spot ER	Six-Month Forward Rate	Six-Month Euro Deposit Rate
6/30/82	BP	1.7340	1.7600	13.0625%
6/30/82	US $	—	—	16.1875%
12/30/82	BP	1.6200	1.6140	

hedge the interest paid or received. Table 3.16 contains the exchange rates and Euro interest rates used in the illustrations.

The Synthetic Forward Sale.   Hedgers with exposed assets (receivables, etc.) can design a synthetic forward contract by undertaking the following three steps:

1. Borrow the exposed foreign currency in the amount of the exposed assets
2. Sell the foreign currency spot for the home currency
3. Lend the newly acquired home currency (e.g., place on deposit in a local bank) for the necessary hedge period

On June 30, 1982 a U.S. manufacturer has a BP 1 million receivable in six months. To construct a synthetic forward hedge the manufacturer borrows the BP 1 million spot at the six-month Eurosterling rate, sells the pounds spot for U.S. dollars, and immediately places the dollar funds on deposit earning the six-month Eurodollar deposit rate. The interest expense on the pound borrowing is hedged by selling the proper amount of British pound futures contracts (three, in this case). At the end of the hedge period the British receivable repays the pound borrowing, and interest received on the Eurodollar deposit reduces the net borrowing expense. Table 3.17 outlines the transactions for the synthetic forward sale and compares them with the standard.

Both the synthetic and the standard adequately offset the exposure. In the previous case, coverage by the synthetic amounted to a $4,762 shortfall relative to the standard.

TABLE 3.17. SYNTHETIC FORWARD SALE VS. STANDARD FORWARD SALE

	Dollar Value

Synthetic Forward Sale

June 30

- Exposed receivables totaling BP 1,000,000,
  1. Spot rate = $1.7340 — 1,734,000

- British pound borrowing; borrow BP 1,000,000
  (plus interest) @ 13.0625% for 6 mos.
  2. Estimated interest expense = (BP 65,313)
  [(BP 1,000,000 * .130625) (6/12)]
  3. Estimated dollar value of interest expense — (113,253)
  (BP 65,313 * 1.7340)

- Interest expense hedge; sell three
  BP futures contracts; future rate = 1.7600
  Futures value = (BP 25,000/contract * 3 * 1.7600)
  4. Futures value = (132,000)
  5. Futures "premium" =
  [BP 75,000 (1.760 − 1.734)   = $1,950
  6. Less commission @ $100/contract =   (300)
  7. Net futures premium; (5) + (6) — 1,650

- U.S. dollar deposit; deposit $1,734,000 @ 16.1875%
  (Convert pounds to dollars & place on deposit)
  8. Estimated interest earned =
  ($1,734,000 * .161875) — 140,346
  9. Synthetic premium = (3) + (7) + (8)
           = $28,743

- Estimated receivable value (1) + (9) — 1,762,743

December 30

- Receive British payment; repay loan principal
- Value of receivables; (1) — 1,734,000
- Interest earned on Eurodollar deposit; (2) — 140,346
- Interest expense on pound borrowing;
  10. (BP 65,313 * $1.6140) — (105,415)
  11. Futures hedge value; BP 75,000 * 1.6140 = 121,050
  12. Loss on futures contracts; (1) + (4) — (10,950)
- Final receivable value; (1) + (8) + (10) + (12) — 1,757,981
- Change from estimated value — (4,762)

98

TABLE 3.17.   (Continued)

	Dollar Value
Standard Forward Sale	

June 30

- Exposed receivables totaling BP 1,000,000
  1. Spot rate = $1.7340 — 1,734,000
- Negotiate forward sale; forward rate = 1.7600
  2. Premium = (1.760 − 1.734) * BP 1,000,000 — 26,000
- Estimated receivable value; (1) + (2) — 1,760,000

December 30

- Receive British payment; sell pounds to bank at agreed forward rate (1.7600)
- Final receivable value — 1,760,000
- Change from estimated value — 0

Note: "*" indicates multiplication.

The Synthetic Forward Purchase.   A synthetic forward purchase involves transactions opposite to those of the synthetic forward sale. They are:

1. Borrow the home currency equivalent of the liabilities due
2. Using the borrowed home currency, purchase the desired foreign currency in the spot market
3. Place the foreign currency on deposit (where permitted) for the necessary hedge period

This time the U.S. manufacturer has six-month British payables totaling BP 1 million. The manufacturer designs a synthetic forward purchase using the previously discussed guidelines. The manufacturer borrows the U.S. dollar equivalent of the British payable, uses the borrowed dollars to purchase 1 million spot, and then places the pounds on deposit. The interest earned on the Eurosterling deposit is hedged by purchasing the appropriate num-

TABLE 3.18. SYNTHETIC FORWARD PURCHASE VS. STANDARD FORWARD PURCHASE

	Dollar Value
Synthetic Forward Purchase	

June 30

- Exposed payables totaling BP 1,000,000;
  1. Spot rate = $1.7340 ..... (1,734,000)
- U.S. dollar borrowing; borrow U.S. equivalent of BP 1,000,000 @ 16.1875% for 6 mos.
  2. Estimated interest expense ($1,734,000 * .161875) ..... (140,346)
- Interest earnings hedge; purchase three BP futures contracts; future rate = 1.7600
  Futures value = (BP 25,000/contract * 3 * 1.7600)
  3. Futures value = 132,000
  4. Futures "discount" =
     [BP 75,000 (1.760 − 1.734)   = (1,950)
  5. Plus commission @ $100/contract =   (300)
  6. Net futures discount; (4) + (5) ..... (2,250)
- Eurosterling deposit; BP 1,000,000 @ 13.0625% (Convert dollars to pounds & place on deposit)
  7. Estimated interest earned = (BP 1,000,000 * .130615) (6/12) = BP 65,313
  8. Estimated dollar value of interest earned 113,353
  9. Synthetic discount = (2) + (6) + (8)
     = ($29,251)
- Estimated payable value ..... (1,763,343)

December 30

- Remit British payment;
- Value of payables; (1) ..... (1,734,000)
- Interest expense on Eurodollar borrowing; (8) ..... (140,346)
- Interest earned on pound deposit;
  10. (BP 65,313 * $1.6140) 105,415
  11. Futures hedge value; BP 75,000 * 1.6140 = (121,000)
  12. Gain on futures contracts; (11) + (3) 10,950
- Final payable value; (1) + (8) + (10) + (12) ..... (1,757,981)
- Change from estimated value 5,322

TABLE 3.18. (*Continued*)

	Dollar Value
Standard Forward Purchase	
June 30	
• Exposed payables totaling BP 1,000,000	
1. Spot rate = $1.7340	(1,734,000)
• Negotiate forward purchase; forward rate = 1.7600	
2. Discount = (1.76 − 1.734) * BP 1,000,000	(26,000)
• Estimated payable value; (1) + (2)	(1,760,000)
December 30	
• Remit British payment; purchase pounds from bank at agreed forward rate (1.7600)	
• Final payable value	1,760,000
• Change from estimated value	0

Note: "*" indicates multiplication.

ber of futures contracts. Again, the interest earned on the pound deposit will help to offset the Eurodollar borrowing expense. Table 3.18 details the synthetic forward purchase transactions and compares them to the standard.

In these two cases, the synthetic forward hedge produced nearly the same outcome as the standard. The difference in cost between the two amounted to approximately plus or minus $5,000, or only 0.2 percent of the total exposure value.

NOTES

1. Based on an analysis in Antl, Boris, (ed.). *The Management of Foreign Exchange Risk.* London: Euromoney (1980) 58−61, 74−75.

2. Antl, Boris (ed.). *Currency Risk and the Corporation.* London: Euromoney, (1981) 50−51.

3. Ibid.

4. Bear, R.M. *Introduction to Futures Contracts, The Handbook of Financial Markets.* Dow Jones-Irwin, 1981, 629−630.

5. IMM Foreign Exchange Daily Information Bulletin, International Monetary Market, 3/16 and 9/17 1984.

6. Fama, E. "Forward Rates as Predictors of Future Spot Rates," *Journal of Financial Economics* (October 1976): 361–378. Kaserman, R. "The Forward Exchange Rate; Its Determination and Behavior as a Predictor of the Future Spot Rate," Proceedings of the American Statistical Association, 1973. Kettell, B. "The Forward Rate as a Accurate Predictor of Future Spot Rates," *Managerial Finance* 4, no. 2 (1978): 131–142.

7. In an efficient market (strong form), all information, public and private, is assumed to be fully reflected in the exchange rate. This is highly improbable in foreign exchange markets where exchange rates are at times quietly manipulated by heads of governments.

8. Soenen, L.A., and Van Winkel, E.G.F. "The Real Costs of Hedging in the Forward Exchange Market," *Management International Review* 22: 56–58.

9. Bear, R.M. *Introduction to Futures Contracts.*

10. There are many variations, some highly involved, of the simple hedge ratio calculation presented here.

11. Gay, Gerald D., and Kolb, Robert W. "The Management of Interest Rate Risk," *Journal of Portfolio Management* (Winter 1983).

12. Hill, Joanne, and Schneeweis, Thomas. "A Note on the Hedging Effectiveness of Foreign Currency Futures," *The Journal of Futures Markets* 1, no. 4 (1982).

13. Assay, Michael, and Schirr, Gary. "Determining a Hedge Ratio: Two Simple Approaches," *Market Perspectives* 1, no. 2 (May 1983).

14. A two-week period is required due to the lack of suitable daily liquidity in the PHLX market at this time (June 1983). Options on futures trading on the IMM in Chicago have since been introduced. From their inception these contracts have traded at significantly higher volume levels than their PHLX cousins.

15. This is assuming that one is using American style options. American style options permit exercise at any time prior to the expiration date. European style options allow exercise on the expiration date only.

16. Option premiums are generally priced higher than the futures/forward premiums (the forward or future could even be at a discount) due to the additional value placed on owning the option to exercise.

17. Staloff, A. *U.S. Section/Forex Options.* London: Euromoney (1983): 87.

18. Heberton, L. *Why Buying Over-the-Counter Is a Better Option,* London: Euromoney (November 1983): 87.

4

A Tax Management Recap

Understanding the tax laws as they apply to hedging foreign exchange is crucial to the evaluation and subsequent refinement of the hedge. In Chapter 2 we demonstrated that hedging an exposure that has not been measured from an after-tax viewpoint can lead to excessive hedging. Moreover, once the taxation of the exposure is considered one can still risk *underhedging* if the tax consequences pertaining to the hedge itself are not addressed as well. Thus taxation enters the hedging process on two fronts. First, and as described in Chapter 2, it is necessary to calculate the amount of after-tax exposure. Second, if the exposure is to be protected by a hedging transaction, the amount required for the hedge must also be determined from an after-tax perspective. Depending on the nature of the exposure, gains and losses on the hedge may be subject to varying tax rates.

There is a surprisingly limited collection of information and legislation dealing specifically with the taxation of foreign exchange hedging transactions. Consequently, most decisions are still based on the outcome of a handful of past, and by now well known, tax court decisions.[1] From these earlier cases some broad guidelines have evolved, and we introduce them, in brief, in the following sections. We stress, however, that the tax considerations presented are merely an introduction. The authors recommend consulting tax experts prior to making any hedging decision that may be influenced by this complex and ever changing field.

TAX CONSIDERATIONS PRIOR TO HEDGING

Two fundamental tax areas should be considered before entering a hedging transaction. First, the question arises as to whether the gain or loss on the hedge will be characterized as ordinary or capital. In most cases the treatment depends on the relationship of the gain or loss to the firm's trade or business.[2] Hedges of normal business activities such as payables or receivables, inventory, or other assets and/or liabilities associated with the firm's daily operations are generally considered to be ordinary. On the other hand, gains or losses on hedges intended to protect a capital asset, say an investment in a foreign subsidiary, would generally be treated as capital.[3] A second concern to the hedger is the source of the gain or loss. That is, is the gain or loss foreign or domestic? Where settlement of a forward type contract results in a foreign exchange gain, the source is generally determined to be where the ownership of the currency is transferred. For instance, if the currency is transferred to an entity in a foreign country via a bank in that country the source should be foreign. However, capital gains are almost always recharacterized as domestic source, except in those cases where the gain is subjected to a foreign income tax of at least 10 percent of the gain.[4] The sourcing of losses is tied to the relationship of the loss to the class of income generated by the asset or liability being hedged. Other factors that may influence characterization are the holding period, the timing of the gain or loss, and if hedging is undertaken in a foreign nation, any local tax laws that may apply.

Arranging, when applicable, for taxation of the hedge at the lower rate (relative to the exposure) benefits the hedger in two ways. First, the taxation of the gain or loss on the hedge is lower. And second, the size of the hedge required to offset the exposure is less. The result is a potential lowering of the basic cost of the hedge.

AFTER-TAX HEDGING

There are three general steps to hedging from an after-tax perspective:

1. Find the after-tax exposure.
2. Using the after-tax exposure value, determine the after-tax amount of required hedge.
3. Employ the hedge.

Let us upgrade the forward and futures contract examples of Chapter 3 to bring taxes into the hedging process.

Step 1.   Refer back to Chapter 3 and the U.S. manufacturer with payables totaling BP 1 million. If the payables are determined to be a part of the firm's normal operations they would probably be subject to the ordinary U.S. tax rate (we'll use 46 percent). First, we find the after-tax (AT) exposure (Eq. A, Table 2.3):

$$
\begin{aligned}
\text{AT exposure} &= \text{Pre-tax exposure} * (1 - \text{present tax}) \\
&= \text{BP } 1{,}000{,}000 * (1 - .46) \\
&= \text{BP } 540{,}000
\end{aligned}
$$

The after-tax value of the British payable exposure is BP 540,000, considerably less than the pre-tax amount.

Step 2.   The gain or loss on a forward contract type hedge is expected to offset any corresponding loss or gain on the exposure. But gains and losses on such hedges are taxable. Thus taxing the gain or loss on the hedge erodes the final amount of offset. The value of the hedge must be adjusted to compensate for any perceived tax effects. The total amount required for corresponding full cover can be found by using Equation 4.1.

$$
\text{AT full hedge} = \text{AT exposure} * [1/(1 - \text{hedge tax})] \quad (4.1)
$$

If the gain or loss on the hedge is also regarded as ordinary (as would be the case for most day-to-day hedges), income on the hedge should be taxed at the 46 percent rate too. So, in this case the tax on the hedge would offset the tax on the exposure. The after-tax amount of BP that must be bought forward for full protection equals the pre-tax exposure:

$$\text{AT full hedge} = \text{BP } 540{,}000 * [1/(1-.46)]$$
$$= \text{BP } 1{,}000{,}000$$

In this case, tax affecting the hedge returns the after-tax exposure (or the amount required for full cover) back to BP 1 million. The tax effect on the hedge perfectly offsets the tax impact on the exposure.

Step 3. Recall that on March 16 the manufacturer hedges by entering a forward purchase contract for the six-month period ending September 17. Since the after-tax hedge is BP 1 million, the final outcome of this hedge mirrors the example in Chapter 3 (see Tables 3.3 and 3.4).

When Tax Rates Differ

Suppose, however, that the manufacturer expects that it can arrange capital gains treatment on the hedge, even though the exposure is deemed ordinary. If this were true, income on the hedge would be taxed at the capital gains rate (28 percent in the United States). The total after-tax amount of British pounds that must be purchased forward is:

$$\text{AT full hedge} = \text{BP } 540{,}000 * [1/(1-.28)]$$
$$= \text{BP } 750{,}000$$

The capital gains tax rate is lower than the ordinary rate, thus the amount required for full cover does not increase as sharply. Here, the required hedge is BP 750,000, compared to BP 1 million required under ordinary treatment. Calculating the exposure and the hedge from an after-tax perspective places this manufacturer in a more favorable hedging position (contrasted with evaluating and hedging strictly on a pre-tax basis, as done in Chapter 3).

Table 4.1 outlines a previous example in Chapter 3, this time

TABLE 4.1.   MEASURING AND HEDGING EXPOSURE AFTER TAX

		Dollar Value
	Exposure	
March 16:	1. BP payables (pre-tax); 1.4465 * (BP 1,000,000)	(1,446,500)
	2. Tax @ 46%	665,390
	3. After-tax expense (BP 540,000); (1) − (2)	(781,110)
September 17:	4. Value of payment remitted @ 1.2335	(1,233,500)
	5. Tax @ 46% (credit)	567,410
	6. Net; (4) − (5)	(666,090)
	7. After-tax gain/(loss); (3) − (6)	115,020
	Forward Hedge	
March 16:	8. BP purchased forward; 1.4603 * (BP 750,000)	(1,096,225)
September 17:	9. Value of BP 750,000 @ 1.2335	(925,125)
	10. Foreign exchange loss; (8) − (9)	(171,100)
	11. Tax @ 28%	47,628
	12. After-tax gain/(loss); (10) − (11)	(123,472)
Difference between exposure and hedge; (7) − (12)		(8,452)

from an after-tax viewpoint. We assume the same conditions as in Chapter 3. On March 16 the spot and forward rates are 1.4465 and 1.4603, respectively. By September 17 the spot exchange rate has dropped to 1.2335.

A comparison of Tables 4.1 and 3.4 illustrates the effectiveness of hedging after tax. Table 4.1 shows that although the spot exposure (1), before taxes, is $1,446,500, the value of the hedge purchased forward (8), after taxes, is only $1,096,225. In Table 3.4 the amount of pounds bought forward is $1,460,300. Thus accounting for taxes significantly reduced the amount of the manufacturer's hedge.

Reducing the hedge amount lowers premium costs, commissions, etc., associated with the hedge. In the case just discussed the after-tax premium expense totaled $8,452, compared to $13,800 for the pre-tax hedge of Table 3.4.

NOTES

1. *Corn Prods. Refining Co.* v. *Comm'r*, 350 US 46 (1955); *Hoover Co.*, 72 TC 206 (1979); *International Flavors & Fragrances* v. *Comm'r*, 62 TC 232 (1974); *Wool Distributing Corp.* v. *Comm'r* (1978).
2. *Corn Prods. Refining Co.* v. *Comm'r*, 350 US 46 (1955).
3. Effective in 1987, new tax laws adopted by the United States blur the distinctions between ordinary and capital gains. Note, however, that these changes may not apply to foreign countries.
4. Internal Revenue Code, Section 904.

5

Foreign Exchange Controls and Regulations

Many of the techniques of Chapter 3 involve, at least indirectly, transferring the exposure from an area of high risk to an area of low risk. However, the transactions required (borrowing or lending in foreign currency, forward contracts, etc.), ultimately involve the transfer of funds into and/or out of foreign nations. Depending on the countries involved, a variety of obstacles may potentially impede the smooth transfer of funds. Such restrictions are a common element of international business. It is critical that the financial manager be current on the regulations influencing the firm's foreign currency transactions and interests, hedge related or otherwise.

Countries, particularly the lesser developed countries, restrict the flow and convertibility of their home currency to influence trade and reinvestment. Through foreign exchange, governments have the ability to assume some control over the funds that enter, stay, and eventually leave their borders. Their assumption is that without such controls, foreign investors and governments can easily enter an underdeveloped nation and deplete its resources (land, labor, etc.) while contributing little to the actual development of the country itself. Exchange controls are designed to assure that at least a portion of the foreign earnings remain and contribute to the nation's growth.

Foreign exchange barriers take a variety of forms. Broadly categorized, these restrictions are:

1. Restrictions on the remittance or transfer of funds
2. Restrictions on forward contracts (or no forward market at all)
3. Restrictions on trade; these often appear as tariffs, quotas, credit and billing terms (designed to limit leading and lagging), etc.
4. Foreign exchange controls; some governments require or encourage foreign investors to maintain various "non-resident" accounts. The flow of funds into and out of these accounts can then be monitored.

In the following section we briefly review the first two restrictions and list the countries that support related controls. This summary merely highlights common restrictions and the nations that impose them. Complete information on a particular country can be obtained from the firm's foreign subsidiary, major accounting firms, international banks, and government representatives of foreign countries.[1]

RESTRICTIONS ON THE REMITTANCE OR TRANSFER OF FUNDS

Governments attempt to regulate the level of investment leaving the country by placing restrictions on the remittance of profits, dividends, royalties, service fees, interest and loan payments, and so forth. Generally, any funds transfer requires registration and approval by a designated central bank. Often a withholding tax based on a percentage of the funds is levied. The following countries support restrictions in one or more of the areas discussed:

Argentina	Colombia	Greece	Nigeria	Venezuela
Brazil	Denmark	Iran	Portugal	West Germany
Canada	Egypt	Israel	Spain	Zaire
Chile	France	Italy	Taiwan	

RESTRICTIONS ON FORWARD CONTRACTS
(OR NO FORWARD MARKET)

Governments may restrict forward contract maturity dates, the types of banks where they are accessible, and the types of transaction in which forward cover is permitted. Countries with a relatively restrictive forward market are:

Argentina	Chile	Indonesia	Panama	Venezuela
Australia	Colombia	Iran	Portugal	Zaire
Bahamas	France	Mexico	Republic of Korea	
Brazil	Hong Kong	Nigeria	Taiwan	

COUNTRIES WITH FEW FOREIGN EXCHANGE RESTRICTIONS

A number of countries operate with few or no foreign exchange restrictions at all. Judging by the list, these countries are typically the more industrialized nations whose currencies are considered strong.

Austria	Malaysia	Singapore	United States
Belgium	Mexico	Sweden	West Germany
Canada	Netherlands	Switzerland	
Finland	Norway	Thailand	
Japan	Panama	United Kingdom	

The majority of these currencies of countries imposing few restrictions also appear in a list of currencies found to be commonly used by U.S. companies. This list, in Appendix 7, was generated by the corporate hedging survey detailed in Chapter 6.

NOTES

1. A limited description of country exchange restrictions can be found in: *Price Waterhouse Information Guide*, "Current Foreign Exchange Information, A World Wide Summary." New York: Price Waterhouse, 1982; George, Abraham M. *Foreign Exchange Management and the Multinational*, New York: Praeger, 1978.

6

Corporate Hedging Survey

Hedging foreign exchange risk has become a matter of growing concern among banks, corporations, and individual traders. Violently fluctuating exchange rates are forcing corporations and traders to become more thorough in the analysis and protection of their currency exposures. New hedging tools such as currency options, along with scores of publications offering innovative hedging strategies, are representative of this new, heightened awareness. With so much information at hand and more in the offing, it is ironic that little of it has addressed what is actually happening within the corporation and its hedging operations.

This dearth of information led CISCO, a Chicago futures research firm, to undertake a hedging survey in 1984 of Chicago-area companies. The survey's principal aim was to examine, in general, the current state of corporate foreign exchange hedging. That is, who is hedging, why, what is being hedged and how it is being done. Do companies have all the bases covered, or are they still learning to play the game?

THE PARTICIPANTS

The survey sample was drawn from the 211 largest nonfinancial companies in the Chicago area.[1] Regional banking and insurance and utility companies were excluded. This sample is especially useful because of its diversity in both firm size and industry. Of the 159 companies asked to participate, 56, or 35 percent, responded. Total sales of the solicited firms ranged from $30 billion to $9.5 million.

Introductory questions explored the general background of each respondent so that they could be grouped and evaluated properly. Two factors in particular were thought to be critical to the hedging analysis: first, whether or not a firm engages in foreign exchange transactions at all, and second, the approximate size of the exposure.

Two-thirds of the responding firms stated that they engaged in foreign currency denominated transactions and/or held overseas assets. And as mentioned previously, the hedgers were separated based on the size of their exposures, to find the effect of exposure size on hedging activity or the protective method used. An exposure equivalent to $1 million was selected as the dividing point between large and small hedgers. One million dollars is the approximate size of acceptance for forward contracts arranged through banks and the range where futures contracts become too cumbersome and expensive (relative to forwards) due to contract size. Of the respondents with foreign exchange transactions, 57 percent said their exposures were, on the average, greater than $1 million. Approximately 70 percent of the firms having large exposures would also be considered *large* firms and vice versa for companies with exposures of the smaller amount. This classification is based on the total assets of all firms in the survey sample. Because the mean is distorted by a few very large companies, the median value ($105 million) is chosen as the separation point between large and small firms.

HEDGING APPROACH

Three-quarters of the group with foreign currency transactions hedged their exposures. Earlier, we found the participants evenly divided in terms of exposure size. Of the participants that hedged, however, the large hedgers outnumbered the small by a ratio of two to one. Nonhedging respondents (24 percent) do not hedge for a variety of reasons. Two-thirds of this group claimed that their exposures balanced each other out, 22 percent cited company policy, 22 percent cited other reasons, and one respondent stated that the costs outweighed the benefits.

Several factors serve as indicators of the basic hedging approach. The firms' intended policy towards hedging, hedging objectives, techniques used, and forecasting information are useful in defining the nature and complexity of the firms' hedging operations. When asked if a hedging policy had been defined by their board of directors, more than 80 percent of the firms with foreign currency exposures stated that they did not have an official hedging policy. This finding indicates that the perceived importance of hedging has, generally, not reached a level warranting official recognition by the board.

Companies' perception of the foreign exchange market and its associated risks can probably best be learned by looking at their hedging objectives. The hedgers were asked to classify these objectives in one of the following categories: minimize losses, come out even, and minimize losses but take advantage of potential exchange gains. The first two categories are considered conservative hedgers; the third is the more aggressive. As a group, 57 percent aimed to minimize losses or come out even (conservative). The remaining hedgers also wanted protection but recognized the potential for exchange gains. A 1977 survey conducted by the Center for Multinational Studies in Washington, D.C.[2] showed similar results, that is, the principal hedging objectives of multinationals were conservative.

The participants were given a list of hedging methods and asked to indicate which techniques they used in their program (see Table 6.1). The results shed light on which methods are used most frequently, the general level of acceptance of newer methods, and the influence of exposure size on the method used. Nearly three-quarters (71 percent) of all respondees used internal techniques and most (96 percent) employed external measures of some kind. Forward contracts were most often used (96 percent) by the same group. Currency futures were the only other external method used by more than 10 percent of the hedgers. Two factors, speciality and

TABLE 6.1.   HEDGING TECHNIQUES LISTED IN THE SURVEY
                            QUESTIONNAIRE

Forward foreign exchange contracts	26	93%
Futures contracts	3	11%
Bank foreign exchange options	2	7%
Exchange-traded foreign exchange options	1	—
Internal corporate techniques	20	71%
Technically oriented hedging methods	1	—

unfamiliarity, probably contribute to the relative lack of use of the
other methods. Bank and exchange options are designed, and
therefore, most useful with specific types of transactions. Moreover, both options and technical methods are still relatively new to
currency hedging. Currency futures, however, are not nearly so recent. Thus unfamiliarity with futures does not explain their lack of
use, particularly since there are few fundamental differences between forward and futures contracts. A strong bank/corporate relationship may be one reason why forwards are preferred to futures
(97 percent of the respondents rely on their bank for foreign exchange information). Banks provide additional services in the form
of exchange rate forecasts, positioning advice, and so forth. Futures
exchanges and many brokerage houses do not. Also, the smaller,
standardized size of the futures contract limits its use for the larger
hedger. Lastly, futures contracts are only available in selected currencies, namely the British pound, Canadian dollar, yen, mark, and
Swiss franc (with exception to "basket" currencies such as the European Currency Unit and the U.S. Dollar Index). Forwards, on the
other hand, can be negotiated in virtually all currencies, from the
more common to the exotic, if the price is right. Note that the se-
lectivity of currencies is certainly a contributing factor to the relative disuse of bank and exchange options as well. The five major
currencies just discussed are presently the only currencies with option counterparts on U.S. exchanges.

An additional survey question probed the forward/futures disparity a bit further. Respondents were asked to rate the forward and
futures markets (good, fair, or poor) based on the technique's ability to properly hedge the exposure. Seventy-five percent of those

rating forward contracts rated them *good* with the remainder giving them a *fair* mark. In contrast, only 30 percent of the respondents judging futures contracts gave futures a *good* rating; the remainder rated them *fair*. Similar ratings were received from hedgers assessing both forward and futures contracts. The futures market received the same marks, 30 percent good and 70 percent fair. The forward market was split, 50 percent good and 50 percent fair.

The hedgers were asked how often they evaluated their foreign exchange forecasts. About one-third evaluated their forecasts on a daily or weekly basis and nearly 85 percent did so at least each month. Assuming that companies make some sort of forecast prior to placing a hedge, these results may also be viewed as an indicator of general hedging activity. In addition, nearly 40 percent of all hedgers used methods to *time* the placement of their hedges. More than 90 percent of those that timed their hedges conducted their analysis in-house and almost half of the same group used outside timing services as well.

Lastly, all of the respondents were asked if they were aware of educational programs designed to promote hedging tools and strategies. Less than 30 percent were aware of these services. These figures improved only slightly when measured among the respondents with foreign exchange transactions (38 percent). When measured among hedgers (large and small) the results remained, surprisingly, unchanged (38 percent aware, 56 percent unaware). Note that this question may reflect the individual addressing the questionnaire and not necessarily the company as a whole.

INFLUENCE OF EXPOSURE SIZE

Less than 10 percent of the respondents with large exposures (exceeding $1 million) were nonhedgers, compared to 44 percent of the participants with exposures less than $1 million. Thus in this sample, smaller firms were much less likely to hedge their exposures. The majority of these respondents (71 percent) indicated that they did not hedge because their "exposures balanced each other out." These companies may not actively address the exposure problem because they lack the asset foundation necessary to use effectively many internal methods and/or lack the expertise of the larger, more frequent hedger.

The policy question investigated earlier is reapplied here to large and small hedgers. While only one-fourth of all hedgers had an official hedging policy defined by their board, more than 85 percent of these were of the larger type. Thus the larger hedgers were more inclined to define their hedging policy. Note, however, that this group still only accounted for approximately 20 percent of all hedgers surveyed.

Perhaps the most striking difference between large and small hedgers was in how they perceived the hedging function. Small hedgers appeared much more conservative than large hedgers in terms of their hedging objectives. One-third of the smaller variety stated that their principal objective was to "minimize losses" and nearly 80 percent aimed to either "minimize losses" or "come out even." On the contrary, more than half of the larger hedgers aimed to take advantage of potential exchange gains, while only 22 percent of the smaller hedgers were of the aggressive type. These results are interpreted graphically in Figure 6.1.

Figure 6.1 further illustrates the difference in objectives between large and small hedgers. As the *objective* moves from conservative to aggressive, the large aggressive hedgers decidedly outnumber the small.

Large hedgers also used a greater variety of hedging techniques. Eighty-nine percent of this group took advantage of bank forward contracts, 16 percent made use of the futures market and 79 percent employed internal methods. Options and technical methods saw limited use. It is interesting to note that no small hedger claimed to use currency futures as a protection method. One would expect that hedgers with smaller exposures would be more inclined to use the smaller, more accessible futures contracts (as opposed to forwards). In fact, all companies with exposures under $1 million utilized forward contracts. The only other measures employed by the smaller hedgers were the internal techniques (56 percent).

Finally, large hedgers evaluated their foreign exchange forecasts more often than small hedgers. Daily or weekly evaluations were made by 42 percent of the large hedgers versus 13 percent of the

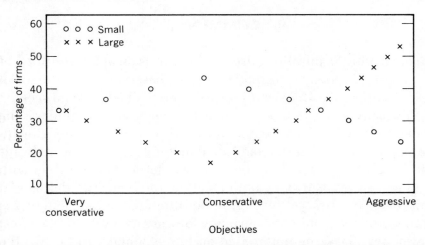

Figure 6.1. Hedging objectives of large and small hedgers. The vertical axis represents the percentage of the group, large (x) or small (o), exhibiting the shown hedging objectives.

small. Moreover, half of the large respondents also used *timing* tools to help place their hedges. Only one of nine small hedgers used such methods.

Several interesting points were produced by the hedging study. (1) Hedgers, both large and small, were typically conservative in their hedging objectives, the majority aiming to minimize foreign exchange losses or break even. (2) Three-quarters of all potential hedgers undertook hedging in some form, yet very few maintained an official hedging policy. (3) Companies with large exposures were twice as likely to hedge as those with small exposures. (4) Large hedgers exhibited a more active hedging program. These firms tended to use a greater variety of techniques, evaluated their forecasts more frequently, and were more apt to time the placement of their hedges. (5) Most potential hedgers were not aware of the educational hedging programs available to them.

An intriguing finding uncovered by the survey is that small companies, the concerns that have the most to lose by not hedging, were the least likely to hedge. Small firms may negotiate only a few foreign exchange transactions each year, therefore they can least afford to have their profit margins wiped out by exchange rate fluctuation.

COMMENT

The old saying "a burnt dog dreads the fire" is an apt description of the majority of today's currency hedgers, based on the evidence of these findings. This bias tends to preclude the hedger from seeking or using any but the most standard of hedging techniques. The rapid currency fluctuations of today and the rise of new hedging instruments suggest that the traditional methods are no longer always best. Futures contracts have been proven to be very effective with small exposures. Currency options allow the hedger to define and limit his or her risk yet further. In addition, technical modeling is gaining credence; only one currency forecasting model in the latest *Euromoney* magazine poll[3] relied on fundamentals, and it was the least profitable of the eight reviewed.

There was a time, even after Bretton Woods and the period of fixed exchange rates, when currency fluctuations were small and of little concern to the financial manager. Over recent years, however, these placid times have disappeared as the erratic behavior of the foreign exchange markets has opened eyes and rattled brains in companies in every corner of the world. If all of the other troubled areas are set aside (labor and production costs, etc.), we find that foreign exchange risk is the added dimension that presently places many companies at a distinct disadvantage to their foreign competitors. That is, a contract negotiated today in dollars becomes a potentially very expensive deal relative to the same contract denominated in, say, deutsche marks. There is salvation, however, for the firm that finds itself in this position. A well-constructed hedge can allow the U.S. firm to negotiate in deutsche marks also. This tactic effectively dissolves the firm's foreign exchange risk and places the concern head to head with the competition. Improvements in the other troubled areas can then be explored and put into action.

Clearly, the successful hedger must become familiar with all the possible alternatives. Moreover, the firm must identify itself within the various classes (ultraconservative, conservative, aggressive, or some combination) so that levels of risk can be defined and understood. With this in hand, a consistent, definitive hedging policy can be developed and should be followed religiously. It is important to stress here that even the most conservative firm should not limit itself to just the most established hedging methods. All the tools (internal account management, forward currency hedging through banks, forward contracting, contracting denominated in the *home* currency, futures hedging, options hedging, etc.) should be developed, understood, and applied as needed. The increased complexity in this field is giving rise to a new class of service organization, a sampling of which is identified in the *Euromoney* annual poll. From the survey, it is clear that most companies are very reluctant to discuss their currency hedging with *outsiders*. However, we feel that, given the increasing need and complexity, exposure management is developing to the point that outside help (as in accounting, law, etc.) is becoming a necessity. At the same time it is important for companies to build up their own competence to ensure optimum interaction with their advisors.

For those businesses that do not hedge at all, failing to hedge an open exposure in volatile and erratic foreign exchange markets is tantamount to speculation. In today's world this is not too far removed from Russian roulette.

NOTES

1. A. G. Becker Guide to The Largest Insurance and Diversified Financial Companies in Chicago, 1983.
2. Evans, Thomas G., and Folks, William R., Jr. *Contemporary Foreign Exchange Risk Management Practices at U.S. Multinationals.* Occasional Paper No. 10, Washington D.C.: Center for Multinational Studies, October 1979.
3. Jacobs, Richard. "Getting It Right At The Right Time." *Euromoney* (August 1984): 148ff.

Part 2

Converting Risk to Profit

INTRODUCTION

In the preceding chapters we have discussed why to hedge, what to hedge, and what to hedge with. Back during the times of Bretton Woods (pre-1973), when exchange rates fluctuated at most by 2.5 percent annually, this information was sufficient to manage a safe, successful hedge. But nowadays, as exchange rates sometimes run rampant and against all fundamental reasoning, the information of previous chapters is not always enough. Knowing *when* to place the hedge is critical. This knowledge is called *timing*. Timing a hedge is somewhat like rowing a boat. Strength alone does not make a good oarsman; timing and technique are required too. Similarly, while the typical hedger will probably keep the exposure within bounds, the hedger using timing stands to gain more for the same effort.

The balance of this book is devoted to the methods for strategically placing the hedge. Foreign exchange futures will play a large role in our discussions because these instruments are priced in a free market (by auction). Forwards and options are covered to a lesser degree. Five major currencies are traded on the currency futures and options exchanges (British, Canadian, German, Swiss, and Japanese). Our work will generally deal with this group. We examine several hedging approaches. Most rely on market timing, which normally comes from a trading model. The exception, the hedge-and-hold, places a hedge the moment the exposure is created and holds until the transaction is completed. As we noted in Chapter 3 this type of hedging is sometimes very expensive in terms of lost opportunity. The modified hedge-and-hold will delay placing the hedge until the timing is proper. Last, a technique that attempts to take advantage of market volatility is the selective hedge. Risk on an individual hedge increases from hedge-and-hold to selective, with the former always entailing commission costs and the latter sometimes providing windfall profits.

Hedging decisions can come from either the fundamental (basic economic) side or from technical analysis. The fundamentals are hard to know in their entirety because the players do not like to show their hands. Still, it is important to have an overview of the ultimate sources of money movements. Timing is more the province of technical analysis, which we detail in Chapter 8. We cover technical analysis and its theoretical basis, showing that the random walk hypothesis does not describe futures movements. An eight-year hedging case study on the British pound in Chapter 9 shows that the selective hedge strategy can provide protection and profits together. Then, we introduce the selective hedge as a viable method for hedging a more elusive animal—conditional exposures. Next, we show that technical timing strategies can enhance the profitability of internal hedges as well.

Our reliance on the technical rather than the fundamental analysis is well justified. An article in the August 1983 issue of *Euromoney* evaluated 11 hedge-trading advisory services. The poorest performer was the one fundamental service, which actually lost money over the 1980–1982 period.

It is convenient to have the forwards, futures, and options to hedge with, but what of the firm that does business in currencies other than the "big five"? These *minor* currencies are not based broadly enough to support exchange trading. Still, cash prices are available daily and it is possible to develop timing models with those data. Without a liquid market, the full flexibility of the selective hedge cannot be brought to bear. Cross hedging often provides the solution. We give a case study of hedging the Australian dollar in Chapter 9. Last, we cover the development of a hedging group within a multinational company. While the direct application to hedging needs is obvious, the ancillary benefits of being constantly alert to the vagaries of the foreign exchange markets are probably most important of all.

7
Technical Hedging

$\mathbf{T}$he term *technical hedging* refers to placing a hedge on the basis of technical, numerical reasoning. The timing of the hedge is derived, more often than not, from a trading model, as shown in detail in Chapter 8. We assume that the exposure is known, so the problem treated is to select the type of hedge, the amount, and the timing. The three types of hedge that we will consider are the hedge-and-hold (H/H), the modified hedge-and-hold (M H/H), and the selective hedge (SH). Regardless of which approach is chosen, the size of the hedge is determined by the exposure and any related tax effects (and the hedge ratio if futures or exchange options are used).

GENERAL HEDGING APPROACHES

Hedge-and-Hold

The H/H hedger is one who either wishes to or must hedge the moment the exposure is created. This is the classic form of hedging. Theoretically, at least, the futures markets were developed for the H/H hedger. Many financial institutions recognize the H/H as the only acceptable form of hedging. Grain buyers, for instance, are usually required to hedge their transactions immediately in order to maintain their line of credit. The concept is so ingrained that in Hieronymus' classic book on futures trading[1] the H/H concept is not even listed in the index. The same is true of a slightly earlier book by Arthur.[2]

The basic H/H question is where to hedge and how much. Ancillary questions concern the effectiveness of a hedge. Are the futures markets an effective mirror of the cash (actual) market (assuming futures are used in the hedge)? Is there adequate liquidity? What are the related costs? Since there is no discussion as to whether or not this type of hedge should be implemented, hedging is looked on as a form of imperfect price insurance.

The properly set-up H/H hedge always has a related cost. With futures, it is a commission (about $100 or less per round turn to hedge BP 25,000). For forwards it is the premium or discount. With options the cost lies in the *premium*, that is, the price the option buyer must pay for a put or a call (the put buyer is a short hedger, the call buyer represents the long). An option on BP 25,000, at-the-money, for 60 days (as of January 26, 1984) has a premium of about 2.1 cents per pound or $525. A put is slightly less. There is also a small commission on the option. Similarly, a bank forward on BP 25,000 for two months would cost about $30 (however, banks do not deal in such small amounts). The option appears expensive compared to the futures or forward, but it does double duty. The option works both as a hedge and as a riskless (after the premium), potentially profitable instrument. This aspect was covered in detail in Chapter 3.

Let us take a long hedger, one who has payables in the foreign currency, and work through a typical hedge. At the start of the exposure, a future is bought. Assume that the future tracks the cash perfectly (it does a pretty good job see Chapter 3). If the currency gains, the future gains by the same amount. The hedger is covered. A gain in the future is cancelled by a loss on the cash. Similarly, the short hedger has a loss on the future (the future is sold short for the short hedger) with an offsetting gain on the cash. If the future and the cash do not track exactly there is a possibility of a small gain or loss from *basis shift* (see also Chapters 3 and 8). A hedge using forwards works in exactly the same way with neither a gain nor a loss in either direction of hedge. The forward price is what the hedger gets at the end of the contract. Last, imagine that the long hedger bought a call option. This allows the hedger the choice of buying the currency at the call price. Let us say the cash market goes up. Then the call is exercised and the profit on the call cancels the loss on the actual. On the other hand, imagine that the price falls. The hedger pays the debt in the less valuable currency, with the difference between the premium and the gain from the price drop becoming a windfall profit.

Modified Hedge-and-Hold

The M H/H differs from the H/H in that it admits of a possible delay in the initiation of a hedge. The delay comes from the fact that there are times when it is disadvantageous to hedge. Roughly, markets spend a third of their time rising, one-third falling, and the last third in equilibrium. So it is possible to place a long hedge just about the time the market is falling or to hedge short while a market is rising.

A decision to possibly delay a hedge leads to increased risk, the potential for windfall profits, and the requirement for a decision process that determines when and in what medium a hedge is to be placed. It is the decision process that interests us most because it is intimately associated with the hedger's conception of acceptable risk. How should the decision to hedge or not to hedge be made? One possibility is for the hedger to define the maximum acceptable risk. (In the following, we consistently use BP 25,000 as a single unit since this is the size of a future.) For example, let us postulate an acceptable risk of $1,000 per unit, or about 2.5 percent of the value of the unit. A simple strategy could be: Place the hedge only if the price has moved $1,000 against the position. Once placed, the hedge would be continued until the end of the exposure, regardless of any subsequent action of the market. An alternative strategy is to refer to a trading model for timing, as is done in Chapter 8. If the model is recommending a position parallel to the hedge (e.g., the model is long and hedge must be long) the hedge is taken immediately. However, if the model is contrary to the required hedge direction, no position is taken until the model turns. Using this rule, there will be times when the hedge is never placed and a substantial windfall profit accrues.

Central to the M H/H is the concept of risk and its reverse side, opportunity, as illustrated previously. Determining the acceptable risk very often forces the hedger into an in-depth evaluation of transactions that otherwise would never occur. Setting the strategy brings the hedger into a deeper understanding of the currency markets. This beneficial side effect illuminates an increasingly important aspect of modern business. Currency fluctuations are large, sometimes as much as 20 percent per quarter or more. The firm that understands the behavior of the markets into which it sells or buys is invariably in a superior position to the firm without such knowledge.

The Selective Hedge

Selectively hedging the currency markets is an attempt *to be hedged if the market is going against the exposure and to be out otherwise.* Whereas the M H/H permitted one trade over the life of an exposure, the selective hedge places no limits. The strategy involved complements normal business practices in that it attempts to capitalize on profit opportunities.

Just as with the modified hedge, the acceptable risk must be determined. In this case it is complicated by virtue of the possibility of more than a single trade. There are actually two risks: the acceptable risk for one trade and the maximum risk for all (possible) trades. If the permitted risk for one trade is the same as for all trades, we have merely the modified hedge. Whenever the maximum risk is exceeded the situation collapses to the modified hedge. If the maximum risk is very large, in theory there could be many trades during an exposure.

The possibility of multiple trades makes it imperative to follow a codified model. In fact, the concept of the selective hedge practically presupposes a trading model for timing. Models are available and two successful ones are covered in detail in Chapter 8.

NOTES

1. Hieronymus, T.A. *Economics of Futures Trading.* New York: Commodity Research Bureau, 1971.
2. Arthur, Henry B. *Commodity Futures as a Business Management Tool.* Boston: Harvard University Press, 1971.

8
Technical Analysis and Hedging

After the decision has been made to hedge, the principal question becomes when to do it. If the strategy is to hedge the moment the exposure is known, and the vehicle is preselected, the hedge is placed without regard to market conditions. In all other situations timing is critical to the ultimate success or failure of the hedge. This chapter deals with technical market analysis as one way to develop the proper timing. First, technical market analysis is defined. Then a theoretical basis for technical analysis is developed, the equation of state concept. Next, the random walk theory of market prices and its applicability to futures markets (and by extension to forwards and options) is considered. A brief review of hedge and hold hedging, modified hedge and hold hedging, and selective hedging as they are accomplished by market analysis is also provided. Last, empirical studies and trading models that demonstrate the efficacy of technical market analysis will be discussed. The logical justification for technical analysis is of paramount importance in establishing the credibility of the results of Chapter 8. However, the purely practical minded reader may wish to skip the theory and proceed directly to the models.

TECHNICAL VS. FUNDAMENTAL MARKET ANALYSIS

The description of the market for every currency may be considered to be broken into two arbitrary parts: the fundamental and the technical. In a large sense these parts are the qualitative and the quantitative. The technical, or quantitative, data are strictly numerical: prices paid, volume traded, and open interest. Fundamental market information deals with basic economic items such as balance of trade, interest rates, inflation, taxation, devaluations, and so on, as these affect the value of a currency. Fundamental analysis consists of evaluating all the fundamental information available to predict the market in a qualitative way, arriving at a conclusion, for example, "as of today the yen is undervalued." Of course a second fundamental analyst might not agree. Unfortunately the fundamental factors are known in detail only in retrospect (what government wants to give advance notice of a devaluation?). On the other hand, by necessity the price paid for a currency at a given point in the trading day is absolute. This is the price that a trader or hedger believes fair at that point in time. The study of strings of prices (or volume or open interest) over a period of time has become known as technical market analysis. Properly, technical analysis is totally quantitative, and its analytical techniques are reproducible and verifiable. For instance, a 10-day moving average of the closing price of the March 1984 British pound future as of December 9, 1983 is 1.4541, regardless of who performs the calculation,

The rationale for technical analysis is the same as for fundamental analysis, namely to determine where the market is heading and trade it accordingly. Both fundamental and technical analysts use data derived from basic supply/demand market forces. However, because the fundamentalists know much about the details of the underlying economics they often overlook the amorphous nature of their work. No matter how thorough the fundamental analysis is and no matter how astute its projections, they are of little value unless and until the market follows the projected scenario. Technical analysts do not take positions on the basis of what should happen. They set up a measure of what size movement is significant, and until that movement is detected they see no reason to take a position.

An analogous name for the technical analyst might be *market timer*. The competent technical analyst will define and distill the significant market behavior from the markets' past actions. What size market movement is meaningful? What is the local periodicity of the market, if any? How much noise or random movement is present? If a move is underway, what is its strength? Is is slackening? If so, by how much? All of these quantities are expressed in numbers, in percentages, or in dollars. Anyone using the same techniques will get the same answers. If a particular measure gives poor results, it can be studied and the system modified. In short, these techniques are quantitative and the researcher has absolute control over the methodology.

The technical models discussed in this book are all relatively simple. One reason is that simple models are easier to understand. Another, possibly more important reason is that fairly simple models are used in the real world. Technical market data consist of four prices (open, high, low, and close), sometimes time of occurrence (structures of the days trading), and volume and open interest. Altogether the data have just a few degrees of freedom from the statistical point of view. Generating models that have more degrees of freedom than the underlying data leads to correlation error. If two variables are correlated to a high degree (say, the high and the close), there is little difference as to which is used.

A semitechnical approach, econometrics, has been popular in some quarters. Econometrics works best when the universe being modeled is very smooth, as was the case with the U.S. economy in the 1970s. As fluctuation enters, econometric models start to fail. There is little evidence that such an approach has much to offer the foreign exchange world. In fact, the strong dollar of 1983 and 1984 uniformly surprised the economists, some of whom used econometric models. It should be noted that Michael Evans, credited with creating the discipline of econometrics, was quoted in a *Futures* magazine (July 1985) interview as believing that the macroeconomic model no longer works.

There is a class of market analyst who uses quantitative technical market data, prices usually, but who draws conclusions qualitatively. This is the chart analyst, often called a market *technician*. Recognition of chart patterns tends to be an art rather than a science. It was Hurst[1] who noted that all chart patterns could be synthesized from the superposition of various waves. More recently, Bousen[2] has pointed up the difficulty of reading chart patterns in real time as opposed to analyzing the past. (Note that the *techni-*

cians so often quoted in the market reports are not the technical analysts of this chapter.)

TECHNICAL MARKET ANALYSIS: THEORETICAL BASIS

Today's relatively free currency markets, like other free markets, are controlled by the forces of supply and demand. These forces change over time. In a particular economy the annual inflation rate might move from 5 percent to 11 percent over the period of a year. It could be said that the average rate-of-change is 6 percent for that year (in scientific parlance the velocity, or first derivative, is plus 6 percent). More than likely the inflation rate did not change uniformly by one-half percent per month throughout the year. Maybe it changed slowly at first and then sped up over the last two quarters. In describing the manner in which the rate-of-change (or velocity) changed it could then be said that it was not a constant (one-half percent per month), but that it too had an associated rate-of-change (again, the mathematician would describe the original rate-of-change of inflation as having an acceleration or second derivative term). (Simply, the rate-of-change of a rate-of-change is called acceleration.) These two terms, velocity and acceleration, are enough to characterize most market variables for mathematical purposes. Each of the variables that plays a role in determining the value of a currency may be described just like inflation previously. If all variables were independent one could search out the important ones and solve a series of semilinear equations, arriving ultimately at a dollar value for a currency under each set of conditions. Much of the field of econometrics has evolved around this approach. Unfortunately, life is not so simple. A change in the rate of inflation will very likely affect the interest rate. There is cross-coupling between most of the salient variables. Just how the interaction proceeds, its time delays, and its ultimate effect on price, the prime variable, practically defies description. There are many such interactions taking place between the variables all the time. More than likely many interactions are nonlinear. Notwithstanding the practical difficulties, let us imagine that we could write down the supply/demand equation for a certain currency. We know that there would be terms with velocity components, terms with acceleration components, cross-coupling, and the coefficients of some terms would be dependent in part on some of the other terms. Mathematically speaking we would have a nonlinear, nonhomogeneous differential equation with nonconstant coefficients. Even if we could ferret out all the terms and their relative interactions and write down the resulting differential equation (the fundamentalists' job) we could not solve it in closed form (e.g., by closed form we mean that a three percentage point rise in interest rates would translate to a possible 10 percent rise in the value of the currency). If we can not write the equation down, nor solve it even if we could, what can we do with it? This question lies at the core of many real world problems in science. (We have the same problem describing the air flow over the wing tip of a jet liner. In spite of our lack of mathematical exactness, airplane wings can be designed and planes do fly.) The analyst must use indirect methods to understand the market.[3]

Developing a Technical Understanding of the Marketplace

The general behavior of the market can be studied. Each day that the market trades, solutions to the market equation are generated. The market tells us how many units are traded and at what price. We can get the general flow by examining the price action, and to a lesser degree the volume and open interest action. We find, by observation, that the market track is remarkably smooth. There are few discontinuities (*gaps* in chart jargon) and most of these are small. Market turns are regular for the most part. Prices tend to trade around particular values (equilibrium points) or move deliberately to a new equilibrium point. In Table 8.1 we utilize the Continua Data ™ of Commodity Information Services Co. (CISCO)[4] to compare futures prices year after year on the same basis with little adjustment. The prices are British pounds stated in U.S. dollars, basis the nearest future, from 1975 through 1985.

It is the price that determines gain or loss, but price is implicitly tied to liquidity. The volume of trading and the amount of open interest in a futures contract determines liquidity. A posted price in an untraded market is no more than an estimate. Throughout the

TABLE 8.1.   THE BRITISH POUND FUTURE FROM 1975 THROUGH 1985, USING CISCO CONTINUA™ DATA

Period of Change	Market Characteristics	Duration (months)
9/75 through 2/76	Plateau around $2.00	6
3/76 through 10/76	Drop to $1.62	7
11/76 through 12/77	Rise to $2.08	14
1/78 through 12/78	Plateau around $2.08	12
1/79 through 8/80	Rise to $2.65	20
9/80 through 1/81	Plateau around $2.65	4
2/81 through 2/25	Falling to $1.23	24
3/85 through 8/85	Rising to $1.60	5
9/85 through 12/85	Plateau around $1.60	4

Note: Although Continua™ prices appear different from cash an accurate reflection of market movement is preserved.

following discussion and examples we use price as the determining element for hedging. However, we make the implicit assumption of adequate liquidity to accomplish the hedge at the price listed. In the real world liquidity would be a factor and, if futures are the hedge instruments, rollovers from contract to contract might be required. For our examples, following such rollovers would needlessly cloud the exposition.

Over the 10-year period there were only 7 major changes in the British pound market. From these data one can conclude that the supply/demand equation may behave like some well-known equations in nature. Conceptually we will think of the supply/demand equation of a currency like a function in thermodynamics. A characteristic state variable is the price (P), while the composite net of the supply and demand factors we will call the tendency (T). The equation describing this situation is:

$$P = f(T) \tag{8.1}$$

Or, in words, price is a function of the tendency. For simplification, let us assume that the fundamental relationship is a constant; now we have:

$$P = \text{const } T \qquad (8.2)$$

As the composite supply/demand forces become stronger (demand dominates) T increases and the price rises. As they weaken (supply dominates) T decreases and the price falls.

Now, to compare with a physical system, let us take a gas-filled globe at a constant temperature (say a light bulb at room temperature). The well-known equation of state for this system is:

$$P = \text{const } T \qquad (8.3)$$

where P equals pressure and T is the temperature. Now turn on the power. The tungsten filament begins to heat up, warming the gas in the bulb. T increases so the pressure P begins to rise. After a while the heat added is exactly balanced by the radiative losses from the bulb (it lights our room) and the cooling of the bulb by the air. At this point, the temperature stops changing and the pressure now stays constant. The beginning state (light off) and the ending state (light on at constant T) are called equilibrium points. To get from one equilibrium to the next, we must pass through a transition due to the change in temperature (T). When the light is switched off, the temperature falls and the pressure drops until equilibrium is again achieved. The lifetime of the pressure in a light bulb is diagrammed in Figure 8.1. Looking back at our simplified supply/demand equation (8.2) and at Figure 8.1 we can get a picture of how a very idealized market might behave. In fact, observation shows that markets do act a lot like this, as shown in Table 8.1.

The foregoing argument does not prove that the supply/demand equation for a currency behaves like a thermodynamic system with

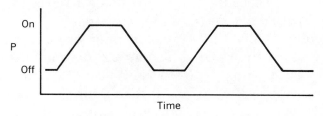

Figure 8.1. Light bulb pressure history over a period of on/off switchings.

state variables. But the evidence does support the analogy. In place of the heating tungsten filament in the bulb we might see the rise in the British pound from January 1978 through August 1980 as heating up the economy, principally because of the North Sea oil. For the pound, the light went out in February 1981 as a result of trade deficits, strikes, a generally poor economy, and so forth.

A review of the other currencies in the manner of Table 8.1 gives the same general result—run, stagnation, and so on. The periods are different, as are the sizes of the runs. We believe that it is impossible to quantify and understand all the fundamental factors that go into the making of a run or equilibrium period. However, the existence of an underlying *equation of state*, with state variables such as price, provides us with a framework for our analysis. It is reasonable to approach a function piecemeal, as we must with an obscure function like the supply/demand relation. On the other hand, if no function exists and the price behavior is random, all the analysis in the world is of no avail. The random walk theory is discussed later in this chapter. But, we will tip our hand by saying that we are convinced that the currency markets' price behavior is far from random.

The Momentum Concept

Once we have established that the supply/demand equation is fairly well behaved and regular we can use that information to extrapolate, or project, the future behavior from the past. This is the momentum concept. In physics it is the first law of motion (bodies in motion tend to remain in motion). In the economics affecting currencies the underlying forces change slowly because of the basic inertia of the system. For example, an increase in productivity often occurs because many individuals in the economy determine over a period of time (during a recession, for instance) that it is to their individual benefit to be more productive. A precept such as this develops over a period of time and does not die out overnight. Thus at any time between November 1976 and December 1977, upward projection for the British pound would have been valid. After a month of uncertainty during which the market was changing direction, an upward projection would have been valid for the ensuing 20 months. To repeat—the structure of the market as determined by the supply/demand equation is regular and long lived, validating the momentum concept. *It is the job of the technical analyst to determine whether the market is trending or nontrending.*[5]

Within the context of a reasonably well behaved underlying structure, the analyst must determine those properties of value in defining the significant parameters. To be able to project properly it is necessary to find any cycles present, to evaluate the *noise* or random component of the market, to find and estimate trends, to determine market direction, and to extract any salient characteristics of that particular market. Since the market may generally be characterized as a small signal buried in a lot of noise, it is rare to be able to unambiguously estimate all properties. Rather, technical analysis is more like applied probability. No measurements are for certain and the day-to-day correlation in most markets is near zero. It should be noted that lack of day-to-day serial correlation does not imply a random market, only that the trend amplitude, when it exists, is usually smaller than the day-to-day noise. The signal to noise ratio is small.

The fact of day-to-day randomness coupled with the observation in the stock market that "technicians" did not fare as well as the market indexes led to the random walk theory.[6] We quote from Malkiel: "The history of stock-price movements contains no useful information that will enable an investor consistently to outperform a buy-and-hold strategy in managing a portfolio."[7] Although currency futures, forwards, and options are not specifically mentioned, the type of market (auction) is the same and we will assume academia feels the same way about futures (a recent book by Gehm bears out this assumption).[8] Such an attitude has serious ramifications in all approaches to market analysis, but none so interesting, practically, as in the evaluation of options. The standard Black-Scholes[9] approach uses the concept of *return* in valuing an option. Return is proportional to the ratio of prices from period to period. But we know from our previous discussion that there are periods of equilibrium. At these times the return calculation will give only a measure of the noise in the prices. We now go to the question of the random walk in futures.

THE RANDOM WALK THEORY

We will start with a paraphrase of Malkiel's definition that was previously discussed: "The history of trading contains no information upon which valid projections of market behavior can be made." It makes sense that if a body of information consists of essentially random numbers, one cannot use that information to predict future behavior. Note that we are discussing a hypothesis, an unproved theory, albeit an important concept to modern capital market theory. Normally, the offering of a counter example to a theory invalidates the theory. In 1973 one of the authors (D. Jones) performed a numeric experiment with futures data relating to the occurrence of new life-of-contract highs and lows.[10] We used the final six months of a contract, covering all active futures in the first nine months of 1972. We examined each case of a new life-of-contract high or low and found that if there is a new high (low) today there is an 80 percent probability that there will be at least one higher high (lower low) within the next 10 trading days. There is a 60 percent probability of two higher highs (lower lows) and a 44 percent chance of three subsequent extrema. Such a high degree of predictability, we feel, argues strongly for the nonrandom character of the market, at least at certain times. In a later section, we show two standard trading models that rely solely on technical data, but have been profitable trading currency futures since 1976.

It seems clear that if one can, from time to time, predict the future course of a market with a high probability (as the chance of a higher high following a new life-of-contract high), the market at that time is behaving in a nonrandom manner. On a broader scale, the profitability of a standard trading model, one that was in existence long before currency futures were created, is the strongest possible argument for the general nonrandom nature of the currency futures market.

HEDGE-AND-HOLD AS A STRATEGY

The hedge-and-hold (H/H) approach was discussed in general in Chapter 7. In this section we will merely discuss the application of H/H and its offshoots. The businessperson who only wants protection from adverse currency price swings and who has a large enough exposure will often purchase a forward contract through his or her bank. Such a contract will guarantee the price of the currency at a future date. This is a classic H/H strategy. The cost of the transaction with the bank will vary according to market conditions. Depending on the market, the cost may be high. Forwards are usually structured for a particular situation and can be very expensive to modify during the life of the contract. An alternative to the bank forwards is the futures and options on the IMM and the PHLX. Futures prices normally differ from the cash currency by the basis. The hedger would enter a futures contract to initiate the hedge and exit when the hedge was to be lifted. Price protection would be total except for changes in the basis. The advantage of the future over the forward is liquidity. The future may be liquidated at any time. Currency options on the PHLX and the IMM offer yet a third hedging vehicle. In this case, the premium or cost is up front. The option differs from both the forward and the future in that once purchased it need not be exercised. This gives the hedger protection over the life of the exposure but if the market moves to the benefit of the hedger the profit accrues to the hedger. The disadvantage of the options market is sometimes a lack of liquidity and rather high premiums. Both options and futures are basically limited to covering British pounds, Canadian dollars, Japanese yen, Swiss francs, and German marks. As noted in Part 1, there are some bank options available, but these are specific to the particular risk. Also, in Amsterdam, options on the guilder are traded, but again the demand is not sufficient to support widespread trading (the guilder was not supported on the IMM, which was also true for the French franc).

Regardless of the instrument chosen (forwards, futures, or options) the hedgers' requirement for price protection over the exposure period is met. But what if the prospective hedger initiates the exposure creating transaction just at a point when the market is going in the hedge direction? There is a good probability of this happening (see Table 8.1). In such a case it would be to the hedger's advantage to delay placing the hedge until the market turned. Then once the hedge is placed it is kept until the end of the exposure. This is the modified hedge-and-hold strategy. To utilize it, one needs the timing tools discussed later in this section.

THE SELECTIVE HEDGE STRATEGY

In the H/H and M H/H strategies the principal aim is to avoid foreign exchange losses. Any profits in the transaction are purely accidental and come from basis shifts. Selective hedging is designed to provide hedge protection while maintaining the possibility of windfall profits from currency fluctuations. Market fluctuation is viewed as a benefit, a potential source of income. Basically, the selective hedger adopts the attitude that currency fluctuations should be handled in such a way that the hedge is on when the market is moving against the exposure and the hedge should be off when the market is *trending* with the exposure. This is a trading hedge where it is possible to make several trades over an exposure period.

The selective hedge requires much more management oversight than H/H or M H/H. Timing and market analysis must be kept up on a daily basis. Management must set risk levels for potential trading losses. On occasion a certain exposure will be traded for a loss; management must understand this as a price that sometimes must be paid. In short, to selectively hedge requires management to treat currency fluctuations as they would any other aspect of their business. The disadvantage of the trading hedge is possible trading losses. The advantages are potential *windfall* hedging gains from being unhedged at the right time and a heightened understanding of the currency markets. It is the latter benefit that recommends selective hedging so strongly to the authors. The currency markets have fluctuated a great deal in recent years and the prospect is the same for the future. If management is to benefit from these market situations the ins and outs of the markets must be understood. The daily requirements of selective hedging forces management to stay familiar with market behavior. Examples of a selective hedge will be shown in a later section.

HEDGING VS. TRADING IN TECHNICAL ANALYSIS

The ideal hedging model would be exactly like the ideal trading model. Both would go long at the bottom (for a long hedge) and both would go short at the top (for a short hedge). For the selective hedge, the ideal model would also pick each significant intermediate peak and bottom. With such a wondrous model the market would be a total captive. Naturally, the developer(s) of such a model would be loath to use it for hedging. They would no doubt trade it, get rich, and turn to other fields. It follows then that the hedging models available fall somewhat short of the ideal. Realistically, the hedger expects to catch the bulk of an adverse move; otherwise, the hedge is a failure.

Conversely, the standard trading model is successful if it is merely profitable. When the British pound was rising from $1.62 to $2.08 (see Table 8.1), for a gain of $0.46 per pound or $11,500 per contract, the trader would have been satisfied with a profit of $5,000 or $6,000. Over the time frame in question, November 1976 through December 1977, there might have been several trades, not all of which were profitable. In fact, for the Keltner 10-day model (detailed later) there were 20 trades of which 10 were profitable. In Table 8.2 we list the trades for that period. Other trading models will perform better or worse over the same period. All have the general aim of maximizing gain, minimizing trading, and holding risk within acceptable bounds. The trading model wants to extract profits while minimizing the probability that a bad run will destroy the portfolio.

If we use a standard trading model for hedge timing it appears that we are using a model for hedging that is not necessarily designed for hedging. Why not develop a pure hedging model? Where does one start? Possibly the best point of departure for a hedging model is a successful trading model. Such a model tends to be safe and to be well researched beforehand. It is attuned to the market in question, albeit not in exactly the manner desired. Modifications must be made to adjust risk to that permitted by the hedging function. Trading must be limited (or alternatively, response to short-term market fluctuations must be damped). Provision must be made to trade only long or short, removing some of the flexibility of a general trading model. In the following section we will go into more detail.

TRADING MODELS UTILIZED FOR HEDGE TIMING

There are two trading models familiar to the authors that qualify to be called *well known* throughout the futures industry. Both are

TABLE 8.2.   TRADES FROM THE KELTNER 10-DAY MODEL FOR THE
PERIOD NOVEMBER 1976 THROUGH DECEMBER 1977

Date In	Price In	Date Out	Price Out	Profit
		Trades Closed in 1976		
917	176.60	1103	166.00	10.60
		Trades Closed in 1977		
1103	159.40	128	172.90	13.50
128	172.90	131	173.50	−0.60
211	173.50	217	173.80	−0.30
217	173.80	415	178.00	4.20
415	178.00	419	178.40	−0.40
419	178.40	519	179.00	0.60
519	179.00	607	178.40	0.60
607	178.40	711	179.20	0.80
711	179.20	719	179.40	−0.20
719	179.40	906	182.70	3.30
906	182.70	907	183.00	−0.30
907	183.00	919	183.20	0.20
919	183.20	921	183.70	−0.50
921	183.70	1019	186.00	2.30
1019	186.00	1020	186.90	−0.90
1020	186.90	1027	186.50	−0.40
1027	186.50	1028	187.70	−1.20
1028	187.70	1121	190.30	2.60
1121	190.30	1205	191.40	−1.10

Note: See the section entitled Trading Models Utilized for Hedge Timing for details of the
model. As before, CISCO Continua™ data is the source (Jones, D.L., and Strahm, N. "Another Continuation Chart Solution." *Futures* 12, No. 11 (1983): 90 ff).

based on moving averages. The first of these was formulated by
Chester Keltner, a long-time grain analyst headquartered in Kansas
City, Missouri.[11] This channel trader relies on a moving average of
the last 10 days' high, low, and close, a total of 30 points, to define
the trend line of the market. An upper channel is developed by
adding the past 10-day average high–low range to the trendline.
The lower channel is the trend-line less the average range. A long

THE KELTNER 10-DAY SYSTEM

$$BL = \frac{1}{30} \sum_{10} (C + H + L)$$

$$R = \frac{1}{10} \sum_{10} (H - L)$$

$$UC = BL + R$$

$$LC = BL - R$$

where H = Days High
      L = Days Low
      C = Days Settlement (Close)

Rules: * Reverse out of short and go long anytime the rice trades at or above UC.
       * Reverse out of long and go short anytime the price trades at or below LC.

Figure 8.2. The Keltner trading system.

position is taken when the price anytime during the day crosses the upper channel. The long is held until the price intercepts the lower channel, whereupon the long is closed out and a short position is taken. In Figure 8.2 the Keltner system is summarized.

Based as it is on moving averages, during times of flat, direction-less markets (an equilibrium period) there may be a considerable amount of meaningless trading. Further, there is no guarantee that 10 days is the proper averaging period for any particular future. In Table 8.3 each trade recommended by the standard Keltner model on the British pound since the inception of trading in 1975 is listed. The data used are the *Continua* data referred to earlier in this chapter.[12]

A cursory examination of Table 8.3 leads to the impression of a lot of trades. This is the case. There are nearly 20 trades per year, with half being long and half short. Nearly one trade per month for the selective hedger is usually too frequent. Note that as a trading model, however, the average gain per trade is over $300, before commissions; this is acceptable for traders.

TABLE 8.3.   TRADE-BY-TRADE HISTORY OF THE BRITISH POUND
FUTURE FROM THE INCEPTION OF TRADING THROUGH 1985,
USING THE STANDARD KELTNER 10-DAY MODEL

Date In	Price In	Date Out	Price Out	Profit
		Trades Closed in 1975		
926	201.20	929	199.70	−1.50
929	199.70	1010	202.30	−2.60
1010	202.30	1105	203.20	0.90
1105	203.20	1106	203.60	−0.40
1106	203.60	1110	203.30	−0.30
1110	203.30	1210	199.90	3.40
1210	199.90	1212	199.00	−0.90
1212	199.00	1217	200.00	−1.00
1217	200.00	1219	199.40	−0.60
1219	199.40	1223	199.80	−0.40
		Trades Closed in 1976		
1223	199.80	113	200.70	0.90
113	200.70	114	201.10	−0.40
114	201.10	121	200.80	−0.30
121	200.80	126	201.20	−0.40
126	201.20	210	201.80	0.60
211	201.80	213	201.60	−0.20
213	201.60	218	201.80	−0.20
220	201.80	304	201.30	−0.50
304	201.30	324	192.60	8.70
324	192.60	401	188.00	−4.60
401	188.00	429	184.80	3.20
429	184.80	505	182.20	−2.60
505	182.20	511	184.30	−2.10
511	184.30	514	182.90	−1.40
514	182.90	607	177.40	5.50
607	177.40	624	177.20	−0.20
624	177.20	629	178.30	−1.10
629	178.30	709	178.70	0.40
709	178.70	712	180.30	−1.60
712	180.30	714	179.40	−0.90
714	179.40	721	180.20	−0.80
721	180.20	813	180.50	0.30
813	180.50	817	181.10	−0.60

TABLE 8.3. (Continued)

Date In	Price In	Date Out	Price Out	Profit
817	181.10	819	180.80	−0.30
819	180.80	831	180.40	0.40
831	180.40	901	180.00	−0.40
901	180.00	902	180.20	−0.20
902	180.20	903	179.80	−0.40
903	179.80	916	178.60	1.20
916	178.60	917	176.60	−2.00
917	176.60	1103	166.00	10.60

Trades Closed in 1977

Date In	Price In	Date Out	Price Out	Profit
1103	159.40	128	172.90	13.50
128	172.90	131	173.50	−0.60
211	173.50	217	173.80	−0.30
217	173.80	415	178.00	4.20
415	178.00	419	178.40	−0.40
419	178.40	519	179.00	0.60
519	179.00	607	178.40	0.60
607	178.40	711	179.20	0.80
711	179.20	719	179.40	−0.20
719	179.40	906	182.70	3.30
906	182.70	907	183.00	−0.30
907	183.00	919	183.20	0.20
919	183.20	921	183.70	−0.50
921	183.70	1019	186.00	2.30
1019	186.00	1020	186.90	−0.90
1020	186.90	1027	186.50	−0.40
1027	186.50	1028	187.70	−1.20
1028	187.70	1121	190.30	2.60
1121	190.30	1205	191.40	−1.10

Trades Closed in 1978

Date In	Price In	Date Out	Price Out	Profit
1205	191.40	105	196.40	5.00
105	196.40	106	200.60	−4.20
106	200.60	203	202.30	1.70
203	202.30	216	202.50	−0.20
216	202.50	224	201.80	−0.70
224	201.80	411	196.60	5.20
411	196.60	413	194.80	−1.80
413	194.80	504	191.20	3.60

TABLE 8.3. (Continued)

Date In	Price In	Date Out	Price Out	Profit
504	191.20	508	189.40	−1.80
508	189.40	526	190.40	−1.00
526	190.40	630	192.60	2.20
630	192.60	703	195.60	−3.00
703	195.60	817	203.00	7.40
817	203.00	831	203.70	−0.70
831	203.70	1101	212.20	8.50
1101	212.20	1129	206.20	6.00

Trades Closed in 1979

Date In	Price In	Date Out	Price Out	Profit
1129	195.40	103	200.90	5.50
103	200.90	206	199.80	1.10
206	199.80	319	203.30	3.50
319	203.30	321	205.40	−2.10
321	205.40	418	208.90	3.50
418	208.90	502	208.70	0.20
502	208.70	510	206.70	−2.00
510	206.70	529	207.60	−0.90
529	207.60	608	207.80	0.20
608	207.80	612	209.40	−1.60
612	209.40	731	226.60	17.20
731	226.60	824	226.40	0.20
824	226.40	911	227.00	0.60
911	227.00	926	221.40	5.60
926	221.40	1008	219.00	−2.40
1008	219.00	1107	213.80	5.20
1107	213.80	1207	219.90	6.10
1207	219.90	1211	222.30	−2.40
1211	222.30	125	229.40	7.10

Trades Closed in 1980

Date In	Price In	Date Out	Price Out	Profit
125	229.40	204	231.70	−2.30
204	231.70	219	232.10	0.40
219	232.10	409	225.00	7.10
409	225.00	603	235.50	10.50
603	235.50	626	238.70	−3.20
626	238.70	729	243.10	4.40
729	243.10	806	243.80	−0.70
806	243.80	819	242.70	−1.10

TABLE 8.3. (Continued)

Date In	Price In	Date Out	Price Out	Profit
819	242.70	822	244.60	−1.90
822	244.60	915	248.20	3.60
915	248.20	922	249.70	−1.50
922	249.70	1107	253.10	3.40
1107	253.10	1219	248.30	4.80

Trades Closed in 1981

Date In	Price In	Date Out	Price Out	Profit
1219	237.53	115	240.26	2.73
115	240.26	119	243.15	−2.89
119	243.15	129	240.61	−2.54
129	240.61	310	221.83	18.78
310	221.83	326	221.59	−0.24
326	221.59	615	195.19	26.40
615	195.19	625	192.10	−3.09
625	192.10	812	177.18	14.92
812	177.18	901	176.39	−0.79
901	176.39	916	176.92	−0.53
916	176.92	924	170.35	−6.57
924	170.35	1005	175.05	−4.70
1005	175.05	1015	175.25	0.20
1015	175.25	1029	175.13	0.12
1029	175.13	1208	182.47	7.34
1208	182.47	1229	180.53	1.94

Trades Closed in 1982

Date In	Price In	Date Out	Price Out	Profit
1229	180.53	111	180.45	−0.08
111	180.45	421	168.15	12.30
421	168.15	517	171.66	3.51
517	171.66	716	163.97	7.69
716	163.97	728	162.97	−1.00
728	162.97	818	162.60	0.37
818	162.60	830	161.34	−1.26
830	161.34	922	161.73	−0.39
922	161.73	927	159.40	−2.33
927	159.40	1007	159.79	−0.39
1007	159.79	1019	158.74	−1.05
1019	158.74	1130	150.42	8.32
1130	150.42	1208	148.68	−1.74
1208	148.68	1228	150.19	−1.51

TABLE 8.3. (Continued)

Date In	Price In	Date Out	Price Out	Profit
		Trades Closed in 1983		
1228	161.19	106	159.55	−1.64
106	159.55	208	153.10	6.45
208	153.10	222	151.30	−1.80
222	151.30	314	151.00	0.30
314	151.00	318	148.40	−2.60
318	148.40	331	147.80	0.60
331	147.80	510	155.95	8.15
510	155.95	523	156.84	−0.89
523	156.84	603	155.90	−0.94
603	155.90	624	155.20	0.70
624	155.20	714	153.10	−2.10
714	153.10	727	153.52	−0.42
727	153.52	729	152.14	−1.38
729	152.14	816	150.70	1.44
816	150.70	825	150.40	−0.30
825	150.40	912	150.80	−0.40
912	150.80	914	149.17	−1.63
914	149.17	916	150.51	−1.34
916	150.51	929	149.70	−0.81
929	149.70	1006	150.39	−0.69
1006	150.39	1027	149.20	−1.19
1027	149.20	1222	143.44	5.76
		Trades Closed in 1984		
1228	161.19	106	159.55	−1.64
106	159.55	208	153.10	6.45
208	153.10	222	151.30	−1.80
222	151.30	314	151.00	0.30
314	151.00	318	148.40	−2.60
318	148.40	331	147.80	0.60
331	147.80	510	155.95	8.15
510	155.95	523	156.84	−0.89
523	156.84	603	155.90	−0.94
603	155.90	624	155.20	0.70
624	155.20	714	153.10	−2.10
714	153.10	727	153.52	−0.42
727	153.52	729	152.14	−1.38

TABLE 8.3. (Continued)

Date In	Price In	Date Out	Price Out	Profit
729	152.14	816	150.70	1.44
816	150.70	825	150.40	−0.30
825	150.40	912	150.80	−0.40
912	150.80	914	149.17	−1.63
914	149.17	916	150.51	−1.34
916	150.51	929	149.70	−0.81
929	149.70	1006	150.39	−0.69
1006	150.39	1027	149.20	−1.19
1027	149.20	1222	143.44	5.76
1222	143.44	103	142.65	−0.79
103	142.65	116	142.38	0.27
116	142.38	124	139.59	−2.79
124	139.59	202	141.95	−2.36
202	141.95	308	146.80	4.85
308	146.80	327	145.88	0.92
327	145.88	402	143.49	−2.39
402	143.49	503	141.58	1.91
503	141.58	507	139.25	−2.33
507	139.25	601	139.28	−0.03
601	139.28	612	138.00	−1.28
612	138.00	719	131.57	6.43
719	131.57	726	129.96	−1.61
726	129.96	803	131.40	−1.44
803	131.40	821	129.44	−1.96
821	129.44	1024	120.12	9.32
1024	120.12	1116	123.59	3.47

Trades Closed in 1985

Date In	Price In	Date Out	Price Out	Profit
1116	125.49	130	109.98	15.51
130	109.98	208	108.11	−1.87
208	108.11	227	107.38	0.73
227	107.38	301	104.48	−2.90
301	104.48	311	106.12	−1.64
311	106.12	423	122.55	16.43
423	122.55	509	121.88	0.67
509	121.88	801	138.53	16.65
801	138.53	813	139.23	−0.70
813	139.23	903	136.88	−2.35
903	136.88	920	135.53	1.35

TABLE 8.3. (Continued)

Date In	Price In	Date Out	Price Out	Profit
920	135.53	1107	143.01	7.48
1107	143.01	1119	143.94	− 0.93
1119	143.94	1209	147.03	3.09
1209	147.03	1227	144.95	2.08

Note: The study uses CISCO Continua™ data. (PROFIT of 1.0 = $250)

Optimization

One cure for excessive trading on a model like the Keltner is to lengthen the moving average. We will search for the optimum number of days. The word optimum carries with it the connotation of *best*, where best might be maximum gain over a period of time, or it could mean largest average gain per trade or it could be best winning percentage or least drawdown or a myriad of other criteria. We will settle for *optimum* as being the largest average gain per trade, within the framework of adequate liquidity (several trades per year). In Table 8.4 we list a run through from an 8-day moving average to 80 days in steps of four.

From Table 8.4 we select the 68-day average as optimum. Of the 28 trades over the 6 years (4.7 trades/year) nearly half are winners. For either a long or short hedger there will be a signal two or three times per year. In Table 8.5 we show all the trades for the optimized model, over the years 1976 through 1985.

Referring back to an earlier section in this chapter and the tabulation of the general analysis of the British pound behavior, Table 8.6 compares the trading model results (in Table 8.5) to the information in Table 8.1.

Table 8.7 gets more specific. Here, we compare the actual market move (in U.S. dollar terms) with the performance of the trading model. A breakdown of the total hedge performance for long and short hedgers is also shown.

Table 8.7 shows how the optimized model would handle a trading hedge that followed the model without any other criteria. Columns (1) and (2) compare, in U.S. dollars, the total market move

TABLE 8.4.   OPTIMIZATION STUDY OF MOVING AVERAGE OF
THE KELTNER MODEL (TIME PERIOD 1978–1983)

Days	Trades	Wins	$/Trade
8	126	60	283
12	90	45	402
16	80	23	351
20	68	28	405
24	56	25	417
28	60	23	382
32	58	19	400
36	55	18	387
40	53	16	409
44	47	17	568
48	45	15	630
52	35	14	886
56	35	14	845
60	37	15	798
64	31	15	1016
68	28	13	1145
72	28	12	1106
76	29	11	903
80	25	10	1071

TABLE 8.5.   TRADE-BY-TRADE HISTORY OF THE BRITISH POUND
FUTURE FROM THE INCEPTION OF TRADING THROUGH 1985,
USING THE KELTNER MODEL WITH 68-DAY AVERAGES

Date In	Price In	Date Out	Price Out	Profit
		Trades Closed in 1975		
1219	199.80	1222	199.30	−0.50
		Trades Closed in 1976		
1222	199.30	105	201.40	−2.10
105	201.40	113	200.70	−0.70
113	200.70	119	201.50	−0.80
119	201.50	121	200.80	−0.70
121	200.80	128	201.60	−0.80
128	201.60	305	196.80	−4.80

TABLE 8.5. (Continued)

Date In	Price In	Date Out	Price Out	Profit
305	196.80	728	180.60	16.20
728	180.60	908	178.80	−1.80
908	178.80	1118	173.20	5.60
1118	173.20	1122	171.30	−1.90
1122	171.30	1123	172.90	−1.60
1123	172.90	1124	170.90	−2.00
1124	170.90	1202	172.50	−1.60

Trades Closed in 1977

Date In	Price In	Date Out	Price Out	Profit
1202	165.90	531	177.10	11.20
531	177.10	602	178.00	−0.90

Trades Closed in 1978

Date In	Price In	Date Out	Price Out	Profit
602	178.00	310	198.50	20.50
310	198.50	621	193.40	5.10
621	193.40	1116	205.80	12.40
1116	205.80	1211	208.30	−2.50

Trades Closed in 1979

Date In	Price In	Date Out	Price Out	Profit
1211	197.50	201	197.90	0.40
201	197.90	206	200.00	−2.10
206	200.00	914	221.00	21.00
914	221.00	1119	222.20	−1.20
1119	222.20	1126	218.70	−3.50
1126	218.70	1129	221.30	−2.60

Trades Closed in 1980

Date In	Price In	Date Out	Price Out	Profit
1129	221.30	306	227.00	5.70
306	227.00	421	230.60	−3.60
421	230.60	1119	248.40	17.80
1119	248.40	1224	251.20	−2.80

Trades Closed in 1981

Date In	Price In	Date Out	Price Out	Profit
1224	240.26	130	238.60	−1.66
130	238.60	1008	180.05	58.55
1008	180.05	1015	174.80	−5.25
1015	174.80	1030	177.69	−2.89

TABLE 8.5. (Continued)

Date In	Price In	Date Out	Price Out	Profit
		Trades Closed in 1982		
1030	177.69	113	177.74	0.05
113	177.74	507	173.30	4.44
507	173.30	519	170.00	− 3.30
519	170.00	824	166.24	3.76
824	166.24	827	163.24	− 3.00
		Trades Closed in 1983		
1119	161.80	412	153.14	8.66
412	153.14	614	152.89	− 0.25
614	152.89	624	155.20	− 2.31
624	155.20	627	153.37	− 1.83
627	153.37	1007	152.05	1.32
1007	152.05	1012	150.14	− 1.91
		Trades Closed in 1984		
1012	150.14	215	144.44	5.70
215	144.44	405	142.62	− 1.82
405	142.62	1107	125.91	16.71
1107	125.91	1119	122.91	− 3.00
		Trades Closed in 1985		
1121	122.91	319	111.93	10.97
319	111.93	906	132.78	20.85
906	132.78	920	136.83	− 4.05

Note: The study uses CISCO Continua™ data. (PROFIT of 1.0 = $250)

to the performance of the trading model. This very simple model picks up over one-half of the maximum potential gain. Columns (3) and (4) show the total impact on the hedger's position, for example, the exposure and the hedge combined. We assume that the hedger is either long or short for the entire period and the model's recommendations are followed explicitly. Thus the long hedger takes only the long trades and stands aside during short calls. The con-

TABLE 8.6.   COMPARISON OF GENERAL BRITISH POUND MARKET
BEHAVIOR WITH KELTNER TRADING MODEL RESULTS

Period of Change	Number of Trades	Profit/ Loss($)
During the plateau through 2/76	6	− 1,400
Drop from 3/76 through 10/76	4	3,800
Rise from 11/76 through 12/77	7	5,925
Plateau 1/78 through 12/78	3	3,750
Rise from 1/79 through 8/80	9	7,975
Plateau 9/80 through 1/81	2	− 1,115
Drop from 2/81 through 2/85	19	21,150
Rise from 3/85 through 8/85	1	5,123
Plateau 9/85 through 12/85	1	− 1,013

verse applies to the short hedger. For example, during the British
pound fall of the second period the long hedger reaped windfall
profits totaling $7,850 (market move + trading loss, or 9,500
− 1,650). Likewise, the short hedger netted a shortfall of 4,050
(9,500 − 5,450).

Of course, the hedger would not normally continue trading after
the hedge is placed. There would be hedge risk criteria that would
override the trading model. An example of hedge risk criteria is
given in the next section. The trading model would be used for timing with the initial position being taken as directed by the model. If
the market moved sufficiently against the hedge a loss would be accepted and the next entry utilized. It too might be wrong, but ultimately the hedge would begin to work. A trading model used this
way is a probe for the hedge.

Putting the Results to Test

As an example of the use of the optimized trading model in Table
8.5, let us propose a hedge with the following characteristics:

1. The hedger contracts a debt denominated in pounds. Thus if
   pounds gain against the dollar this hedger will lose.

TABLE 8.7.   COMPARISON OF THE TOTAL MARKET MOVE
WITH TRADING MODEL PERFORMANCE OVER THE
PERIODS OUTLINED IN TABLE 8.1

Period	(1) Market Move($)	(2) Trading Model	(3) Long Hedger	(4) Short Hedger
Plateau	0	−1,400	−475	−925
Fall	9,500	3,800	7,850	−4,050
Rise	11,500	5,925	−4,550	10,475
Plateau	0	3,750	3,100	650
Rise	14,250	7,975	−3,900	11,875
Plateau	0	−1,115	−700	−415
Fall	35,500	21,150	30,423	−9,271
Rise	9,250	5,123	−4,127	9,250
Plateau	0	−1,013	0	−1,013
Total	$80,000	$44,195	$27,621	$16,574

Note: The sum of column 3 plus column 4 equals column 2, since the model reverses and
is always either long or short.

2. The debt is contracted as of January 5, 1979, with a due date
   of June 29, 1979.
3. We will use one contract (BP 25,000) for the example, realizing that the hedge can be in any multiples of one contract
   (or half that, using the PHLX options).
4. A selective hedge is elected.
5. The hedger will follow the model except that the hedger is
   willing to assume risk comprised of the greater of $1,000 or
   the loss incurred by a long trade, since the average loss trade
   on the model is $537 (the hedger wants to enter with the
   model, but is willing to risk more before exiting). While the
   $1,000 figure is arbitrarily chosen here, it is of considerable
   importance to pick the *right* value in a real situation. *Right* is
   tied closely to the hedger's risk level and should always be as
   high as reasonably possible.

Long Hedger Case.   Using the trading data of Table 8.5, recommendations for the long hedger trading under conditions previously
discussed would be:

January 5   The model is already long; hedger automatically goes
              long at 202.80 (the closing price on January 5).

February 1   Model and hedger exit at 197.90; loss is 4.90.
              Reversal short is skipped.

February 6   Model and hedger long at 200.00.

June 29   Liquidate hedge at 217.10. Profit is 17.10.

On January 5 the hedger purchases a contract at 202.80, since the
model is already long (as of November 11, 1978). The model exits
the trade on February 1 at 197.90 for a loss to the hedger of 4.90 (or
$1,225 plus commission of about $100). The short trade (February
1 through February 6) is skipped, of course. However, on February
6 the model (and the hedger) goes long at 200.00. There are no more
trades until the hedger completes his contract obligations on June
29, when the price is 217.10. On this trade there is a profit of 17.10
or $4,275 (net profit is $4,175 assuming a $100 commission). Sum-
ming the two trades, the selective hedger's profit is $2,850 (i.e.,
$4,175 − $1,325). The futures have moved 14.30 or $3,575, and the
cash has moved 14.04 (202.30 to 216.34) or $3,510.

   Thus the selective hedger fell short of the perfect hedge by about
$660. A hedge-and-hold would have netted $3,475 for a $35 short-
fall relative to the cash (the hedge-and-hold could also easily have
been done with a forward contract, the cost being the forward premium or discount). Not hedging at all would have netted a loss of
$3,510. Either type of hedge would have been far superior to not
hedging at all. These results are:

	Hedge Performance	Market Move	Net Gain/Loss (+Commission)
Selective hedger	$2,850	$3,510	−$660
Hedge-and-hold hedger	$3,475	$3,510	−$35
Nonhedger	0	$3,510	−$3,510

Short Hedger Case.   Now let us look at the same situation from the
standpoint of the short hedger (the hedger has pound-denominated
receivables). Trade recommendations under the previously discussed assumptions are:

January 5   Model is long, short hedger stands aside.

February 1   First short trade; model and hedger short at 197.90.

February 6   Model and hedger exist at 200.00; loss is 2.10. Long
             reversal is skipped, short hedger stands aside.

There are no further trades through June 29.

The short selective hedger would have made only one trade, the trade of February 1 through February 6 for a loss of 2.10 (or $525 plus $100 commission). In this case, the balance sheet would read:

	Hedge Performance	Market Move	Net Gain/Loss (+Commission)
Selective hedger	− $625	$3,510	$2,885
Hedge-and-hold hedger	− $3,475	$3,510	$35
Nonhedger	0	$3,510	$3,510

The nonhedger (the gambler) did best, the selective hedger next, and the hedge-and-hold worst.

Comparing the Methods.   Since we do not know a priori what sort of hedger (long or short) we are dealing with, we will average the gains/losses of the three operators both for long and short hedging relative to the ideal hedge.

	Long	Short	Average
Selective	− $660	$2,885	$1,112
Hedge-and hold	− $35	− $35	− $35
Nonhedger	− $3,510	$3,510	$0

In this example the selective hedger was hedged and made money (windfall) on the hedge. The hedge-and-hold will generally break even (less commission costs and basis changes if futures are used). The nonhedger will be even in the very long run if the markets are not moving continuously in one direction.

The swings can be huge and costly in the markets of today if one does not hedge. Only the selective hedger stands to gain (or lose) from the hedging process. This type of hedging treats the market as a potential profit center. The utilization of hedging is clearly an important area for the exercise of management control.

A Return to the Basics. In the previous examples we used the optimized Keltner model for timing. For the sake of completeness, we will now apply the raw 10-day Keltner for our timing. Referring to Table 8.3, the period January 5 through June 29, 1979, recommendations to the long hedger trading under assumptions 1 through 5 would be:

January 5   The model is short, long hedger stands aside.

February 6   Place hedge at 199.80, hedge stop at 195.80.

June 29   Liquidate hedge at 217.10. Profit is $4,225
             ($100 commission).

The long selective hedger had a windfall profit of $715 (from staying out until February 6) in addition to the $3,510 market move absorbed by the hedge. Now for the short hedger:

January 5   Place short hedge at 202.80, hedge stop is placed at
             206.80.

February 6   Model exits short at 199.80, profit is 3.00.
             (Note: the hedger may have elected to stay in the
             trade to 206.80.)

March 19   Model shorts at 203.30. Close of 203.50 is less than
             206.80, the hedger stands aside. The 206.80 point
             represented the hedger's risk acceptance of $1,000.
No further trades through June 29.

The short hedger posted a trading profit of $650 ($750 − $100). Cash prices moved up $3,510, so the net benefit to the short hedger is $4,160. Taking the average of the short and long hedges again, we find ($715 + $4,160)/2 equals $2,438. The hedge-and-hold and nonhedgers would be the same as that previously discussed. In this example the selective hedger made money, just as when using the optimum Keltner. In fact, over this period the standard Keltner performed better than the optimum. We would still recommend using the optimum for timing because of the whips inherent in the standard model during equilibrium periods.

A Second Model

If we do not trust one doctor's opinion, often we go to another doctor for confirmation. For similar reasons, we will examine another widely used trading model to confirm our initial findings under the Keltner system. Called the 4-9-18 moving average crossover model, it has been published by Victoria Feeds Chart Service (now Commodity Trend Service of Boca Raton, Florida) for over 10 years. Three moving averages of the close are calculated each day. If the four-day average crosses over the nine-day, an alert is generated. During an alert up, if the nine-day crosses over the 18-day a trade is signaled for the open of the next day. If the model is short at the time, the long reversal is taken (short to long). If it is already long nothing further occurs except some traders take this as a signal to add another long position. Such a juncture would be an unequivocal long hedge recommendation. Similar trading rules hold for short positions. Figure 8.3 describes the three moving averages trading system; Figure 8.4 illustrates it graphically.

We will look at the 4-9-18 trading for the same period examined previously (January 5, 1979 through June 29, 1979). The model's activity was:

December 12, 1978	Long at 196.30
January 15, 1979	Short at 199.20, gain of 2.90
February 15, 1979	Long at 200.00, loss of 0.80
April 25, 1979	Short at 205.90, gain of 5.90
June 4, 1979	Long at 209.70, loss of 3.80
August 8, 1979	Short at 223.10, gain of 13.40

Long Hedger Case.   Since the model was long as of January 5, the long selective hedger would have taken a position on the first day of exposure. The price on January 5 is 202.80. Assuming the hedger follows the same rules as 1 through 5 in the Keltner example the

Three moving average system

$$MA1 = \frac{1}{4} \sum_4 C_i$$

$$MA2 = \frac{1}{9} \sum_9 C_i$$

$$MA3 = \frac{1}{18} \sum_{18} C_i$$

where C denotes the close

Alert up: $MA1$ over $MA2$.
Alert down: $MA1$ under $MA2$.

Rule: If alert up and $MA2$ moves above $MA3$, reverse from short to long on the open the following day.

If alert down and $MA2$ crosses under $MA3$, reverse from long to short on the open the following day.

Figure 8.3. The three moving averages trading system.

hedger will exit the hedge at the 198.80 (close only) *risk stop* if the model does not remain long. The model reverses on January 15, but the hedger stays hedged since the stop of 198.80 was not touched. The model remains short until February 15, when it returns long. The hedge is kept until January 31 when it is exited at 198.50 for a loss of 4.30 or $1,075 plus commission ($100). When the model goes back long on February 15 the hedger retakes the hedge at 200.50. At this point there is a risk decision to be made: Should the hedger exit at 198.80, the original $1,000 risk point which is now a $425 risk from entry, or set the exit at 196.50 going back to the concept of $1,000 risk on entry? Naturally, a $425 risk appears safer than a $1,000 risk, but that is not necessarily the case. The closer we set a stop-exit to the market the more likely it is to be triggered by market noise. The best rule to follow is to minimize trading for the hedger, within the confines of the selective hedge. We would recommend a stop of 196.50 over the closer one of 198.80 (in this case neither stop was hit by the end of the hedge). The market con-

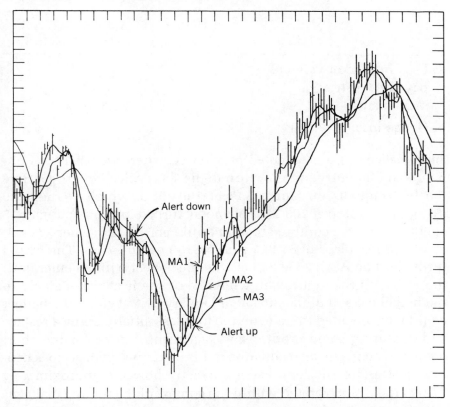

Figure 8.4. Illustration of the three moving averages trading system. An alert up is generated if MA2 moves above MA3. An alert down is signaled when MA2 crosses under MA3.

tinued to move up with the hedger holding the position until June 29. To recap the long selective hedge situation:

	Hedge Performance	Market Move	Net Gain/Loss
1. Entry on January 5, exit on January 31	−$1,175		
2. Entry on February 15, exit on June 29	$4,425		
3. Net on selective hedge (1) + (2)	$3,250		

	Hedge Performance	Market Move	Net Gain/Loss
4. Loss in market value of payable (cash price movement)		$3,510	
5. Hedge loss (3) − (4)			−$260

Short Hedger Case. As noted previously, where we used the Keltner model for entry, we now turn to the short selective hedge. Here
the first entry is on January 15 at 199.20, to which we add 4.0
($1,000) for a stop at 203.20. The model turned long on February 15
at 200.50, but we continue to hold until February 26, when we exit
at 203.30 for a loss of $1,025 plus a $100 commission. The model
turns short on April 25 at 205.90, but the hedger will not enter until
the price returns to levels to which he or she is at risk, namely in
the neighborhood of the 202.50 of January 5. As before, the hedger
could have decided to trade on the turn, essentially doing a restart,
and capturing some profit. The exact reentry price for the short
hedger depends on an evaluation of his or her willingness to accept
risk, just as for the long hedger. Exactly how the approximately
$1,000 risk is interpreted within the context of the trading that goes
with the selective hedge is unique to each hedger, but of overriding
importance to the management of the hedge. In this case, there was
no further decision, since the market continued to climb. Had this
not been the case, the hedger could have possibly taken more than
the single trading loss and in fact could have lost more than the totally unhedged company does when the market moves against its
position. In this case, the hedger started at 202.50 with a need to
cover drops in price. The recap:

	Hedge Performance	Market Move	Net Gain/Loss
1. Entry on January 15, at 199.20, exit on January 31	−$1,125		
2. Gain in market value of receivable (cash price movement)		$3,510	
3. Hedge gain (1) + (2)			$2,385

If we, again, add the long and short hedgers' gains/losses, we find the results for the 4-9-18 model are very similar to the Keltner. The hedge-and-hold loses commission plus or minus small basis changes and the nonhedger comes out even (albeit at high risk). Again, as before, the selective hedger nets a profit of $2,125 ($2,385 − $260). Only the selective hedger is prepared to turn a profit on the currency fluctuations.

Other Models

We have presented results from two well-known models so far because we wish to use models that anyone can reproduce. Of course much more sophisticated trading models exist. Table 8.8 summarizes the results from a total of five models. Two of these are proprietary trading models of Commodity Management Service Corporation (CMSC), and as such, exact details of their operation cannot be divulged. The Keltner H4 is used for guiding customer trading accounts, and a track record registered with the Commodity Futures Trading Commission is available. The Consensus model is constructed from about 20 separate filters and is presently used for special studies such as this one. We provide a performance breakdown over the 1976–1983 period for each of the models in Table 8.9.

The models in Table 8.9 should make it clear that there are adequate approaches for keying hedges. Still, the problem should not be underestimated. There are extensive periods of equilibrium in all markets and selectively hedging in such periods is perilous. (Trading in such periods is perilous, too.) That is why anyone trad-

TABLE 8.8. TOTAL DOLLAR PROFIT FOR VARIOUS MODELS TRADED OVER THE 1976–1983 PERIOD

Model	Swiss Franc	Deutsche Mark	Canadian Dollar	Japanese Yen	British Pound
Keltner 10-Day	58,413	38,813	18,920	62,525	46,310
Keltner Optimized	65,325	32,775	27,510	43,350	32,500
Keltner H4 Optimized	63,575	43,388	28,620	47,750	36,598
MA3TDR 4–9–18	13,901	29,883	23,416	70,769	18,212
Consensus	76,838	50,238	13,588	49,375	24,165

TABLE 8.9.   STATISTICS ON FIVE SEPARATE TRADING MODELS, COVERING FIVE CURRENCIES

	Swiss Franc	Deutsche Mark	Canadian Dollar	Japanese Yen	British Pound
Keltner (10-Day Moving Average)					
Total profit ($)	58,413	38,813	18,920	62,525	46,310
Average profit ($)	1,999	1,430	975	1,720	1,130
Average loss ($)	(674)	(471)	(398)	(439)	(285)
Number of trades	171	175	161	171	151
Wins	64	65	61	64	67
Average trades/year	21	22	20	21	19
Average gain/trade ($)	342	222	118	366	307
Keltner (Optimized Moving Average)					
Total profit ($)	65,325	32,775	27,510	43,350	32,500
Average profit ($)	5,930	2,920	1,488	4,693	3,155
Average loss ($)	(805)	(706)	(364)	(630)	(538)
Number of trades	35	43	71	41	43
Wins	14	15	29	13	15
Average trades/year	4	5	9	5	5
Average gain/trade ($)	1,866	762	387	1,057	756
Keltner (H4 Optimized Moving Average)					
Total profit ($)	63,575	43,388	28,620	47,750	36,598
Average profit ($)	3,296	2,786	1,592	3,936	2,978
Average loss ($)	(783)	(639)	(363)	(740)	(487)
Number of trades	76	50	72	43	60
Wins	30	22	28	17	19
Average trades/year	10	6	9	5	8
Average gain/trade ($)	837	868	398	1,110	610
4–9–18 Moving Average Model					
Total profit ($)	13,901	29,883	23,416	70,769	18,212
Average profit ($)	2,273	1,712	1,479	2,074	1,646
Average loss ($)	(1,548)	(858)	(472)	(924)	(974)
Number of trades	76	73	62	53	72
Wins	38	36	27	33	34
Average trades/year	10	9	8	7	9
Average gain/trade ($)	183	409	378	1,335	253

TABLE 8.9.   (Continued)

	Swiss Franc	Deutsche Mark	Canadian Dollar	Japanese Yen	British Pound
Consensus-Index					
Total profit ($)	76,838	50,238	13,588	49,375	24,165
Average profit ($)	3,374	2,270	952	3,128	2,410
Average loss ($)	(655)	(501)	(392)	(853)	(578)
Number of trades	52	49	75	45	58
Wins	27	27	32	22	19
Average trades/year	7	7	11	6	8
Average gain/trade ($)	1,478	1,025	181	1,097	417

Note: Models Keltner standard and 4–9–18 are discussed in detail in the text. Model Keltner Optimized MA uses a 68-day moving average for the British, with an optimization process similar to that reported in Table 8.4 being performed for the other four currencies. The Keltner H4 Optimized and the Consensus models are proprietary to CISCO (Jones, D.L., and Strahm, N. "Another Continuation Chart Solution." Futures 12, No. 11 (1983): 90 ff.).

ing the previously discussed models at these times is not necessarily successful. The figures relate to the long term, but the trader or the hedger is primarily concerned with the short term—say the last couple of trades. So the hedger must be alert to the market conditions and avoid attempting to hedge in flat, directionless markets. If technical analysis teaches us anything, it is to know the trend prior to taking a position.

SUMMARY

In this chapter we have covered currency hedging as it is accomplished by technical market analysis (TMA). We began by defining TMA as a quantitative mathematical discipline as opposed to the qualitative procedures of chart reading and *fundamental* market analysis. The theoretical basis for TMA proposed an underlying supply/demand function as a driving force for price change. We could not define the exact mathematical equation, but the nature of the market suggests that it is a differential equation with nonconstant coefficients. Conceptually, we liken the supply/demand function to a thermodynamic equation with the price as a *state* variable. The benefit here is that, by analogy, we develop a picture of the market as moving relatively smoothly from equilibrium value to equilibrium value. Such a picture gives the technical analyst a guide to answer the basic question *what is the trend?* The starting point for TMA is the price (and volume and open interest) action, since these data are the continuing solutions to the supply/demand function. We examined the random walk theory, concluding that the evidence of predictable market behavior and the existence of successful trading models disproved the theory. We showed that the selective hedger had the possibility to actually profit from the hedging process. The hedge-and-hold strategy came out even except for commissions and basis risk. (Over longer time periods, the cost of carry can be a significant expense.) The nonhedger will break even over time if the market is fluctuating about some average value. However, the nonhedger faces the risk of the maximum market movement over the life of the exposure. We conclude by suggesting that those who wish to be most conservative follow a hedge-and-hold strategy. Those who view currency fluctuations within the context of general business will be selective hedgers. We propose that the profit potential inherent in selectively hedging active foreign exchange markets will lead many more multinational companies to develop expertise in this area.

NOTES

1. Hurst, J.M. *The Profit Magic of Stock Transaction Timing*. Englewood Cliffs, NJ: Prentice-Hall, 1982.
2. Bousan, R., Jr. "Chart Formations as Optical Illusions." *Futures* 12, no. 12 (1983): 48ff.
3. Jones, D.L. "Blueprint for a Trading Model." *Commodities* 4, no. 4 (1974): 18ff.
4. Jones, D.L., and Strahm, N. "Another Continuation Chart Solution." *Futures* 12, no. 11 (1983): 90ff.
5. Jones, D.L. "The Misbehavior of Commodity Futures Prices." *Commodities* 4, no. 8 (1975): 20.
6. For more information on random walk reports see Malkiel, B.G. *A Random Walk Down Wall Street*. New York: Norton, 1973, 269.

7. Malkiel, B.G. *Random Walk.*

8. Gehm, F. *Commodity Market Money Management.* New York: Wiley/Ronald, 1983.

9. Black, F. and Scholes, M. "The Pricing of Options . . ." *Journal of Political Economics* (1973): 637ff.

10. Jones, D.L. "Predictability of Highs and Lows." *Commodities* 2 (1973): 5.

11. Kaufman, P.J. *Commodity Trading Systems & Methods.* New York: Wiley, 1978.

12. Jones, D.L. and Strahm, D.L. "Another Continuation Chart Solution." *Futures.*

9

Specialized Hedging Techniques

SELECTIVELY HEDGING THE BRITISH POUND: 1976–1985

In Chapter 8 we gave an example of a British pound hedge for the period of January 5, 1979 through June 30, 1979. We examined both the short and the long hedges and found that the net from combining the two was profitable. We pointed out that the trading aspect created risk as well as opportunity and that losses were possible for some exposure periods. In this chapter, we will broaden the inquiry to cover virtually the entire futures trading history of the British pound. We break the period 1976 through 1985 into quarterly hedges to give precise time frames for comparison. There are 40 separate hedges. We assume that the same conditions cover the hedging as before; the following list reproduces rules 1 through 5 from Chapter 8.

1. The hedger contracts a debt denominated in pounds. Thus if pounds gain against the dollar this hedger will lose.
2. The debt is contracted as of the first day of the quarter, with a due date of the last day of the quarter.
3. We will use one contract (BP 25,000) for the example, realizing that the hedge can be in any multiple of one contract (or half that, using the PHLX options).

4. A selective hedge is elected.

5. The hedger will follow the model except that the hedger is willing to assume risk comprised of the greater of $1,000 or the loss incurred by one long trade (if more than $1,000), since the average loss trade on the model is $537 (the hedger wants to enter with the model, but is willing to risk more before exiting).

Hedging with the Optimized Keltner Trading Model

To be consistent, we use the *Continua* data for the input and the 68-day Keltner for timing (again, we could use the standard 10-day Keltner, but opt for the more optimum version because this is the course we would take if we were actually managing the hedge). The hedge period is a calendar quarter, with the starting exposure price as of the close of the day prior to the quarter start (for convenience) and the ending point is the close on the last day of the quarter. If the trading model is already in the market long, the hedge is automatically entered. If the model is short, no hedge is placed until the model turns long. Following rule 5, the hedger may hold onto a hedge even if the model gets out, providing the risk stop (RS) is not hit. For the long hedger, if the model turns short the long hedger will continue to hold long until the RS is hit. At times the model will return long (while the original long trade is still on) without triggering the RS. On these occasions the hedger continues long and, if appropriate, adjusts the RS to reflect the risk on the model's new long signal (per rule 5). Any time the hedge is traded there is an associated *gain* or *loss*. We assume a $100 round turn commission. If a trade is on at the end of the hedge period it is assumed to be traded out at the close of the last day. On the last line of each hedge period there is an item "Market Move" that identifies the dollar amount the market has moved over the life of the hedge exposure (for the long hedger a market drop is a gain, while a loss is associated with a market rise). For instance, for the long hedger, if the market started at 200.00 and ended at 190.00 the market movement would represent a gain of 10.00 or $2,500. There are 40 periods covered by long hedges from 1976 through 1985 that are listed in Table 9.1. Out of the 40 hedging periods, 20 were winners, 7

TABLE 9.1. QUARTERLY LONG HEDGER STUDY OF THE BRITISH POUND OVER THE 1976–1985 PERIOD, USING THE OPTIMIZED MODEL FOR TIMING

Date	Exposure Price	Model Direction	Hedge Action	Risk Stop	Trade Gain/Loss (+ Commission)	Market Move	Hedge Net
1976							
1-02	200.40	Short	No entry				
1-05	201.40	Long	Entry	197.40			
3-05	196.80	Short	Exit		(1,250)		
3-31	191.70		Completed			2,175	925
4-01	191.70	Short	No entry				
6-30	179.40		Completed			3,075	3,075
7-01	179.40	Short	No entry				
7-28	180.60	Long	Entry	176.60			
9-08	178.80	Short	No exit	176.60			
9-14	175.50		Out on risk stop		(1,375)		
9-30	169.10		Completed			2,575	1,200
10-01	169.10	Short	No entry				
11-18	173.20	Long	Entry	169.20			
11-22	171.30	Short	No exit	169.20			
11-23	172.90	Long	Continued	169.20			
11-24	170.90	Short	No exit	169.20			
12-02	172.50	Long	Continued	169.20			
12-30	176.70		Trade out		875		
12-30	176.70		Completed			(1,900)	(1,025)
1977							
1-03	170.10	Long	Entry	164.10			
3-31	178.40		Trade out		1,975		
3-31	178.40		Completed			(2,075)	(100)
4-01	178.40	Long	Entry	174.40			
5-31	177.10	Short	No exit	174.40			
6-02	178.00	Long	Continued	174.40			
6-30	179.50		Trade out		175		
6-30	179.50		Completed			(275)	(100)
7-01	179.50	Long	Entry	175.50			
9-30	184.40		Trade out		1,125		
9-30	184.40		Completed			(1,225)	(100)
10-03	184.40	Long	Entry	180.40			
12-30	200.20		Trade out		3,850		
12-30	200.20		Completed			(3,950)	(100)
1978							
1-03	200.20	Long	Entry	196.20			
3-10	198.50	Short	No exit	196.20			

173

TABLE 9.1. (Continued)

Date	Exposure Price	Model Direction	Hedge Action	Risk Stop	Trade Gain/Loss (+ Commission)	Market Move	Hedge Net
3-23	195.50		Out on risk stop		(1,275)		
3-31	194.60		Completed			1,400	(125)
4-03	194.60	Short	No entry				
6-21	193.70	Long	Entry	189.70			
6-30	194.10		Trade out		0		
6-30	194.10		Completed			125	125
7-03	194.10	Long	Entry	190.10			
9-29	206.50		Trade out		3,000		
9-29	206.50		Completed			(3,100)	(100)
10-02	206.50	Long	Entry	202.50			
11-16	205.80	Short	No exit	202.50			
12-11	208.30	Long	Continued	206.30			
12-29	215.70		Trade out		2,400		
12-29	215.70		Completed			(2,300)	100
1979							
1-02	204.90	Long	Entry	200.90			
2-01	197.90	Short	Exit		(1,850)		
2-06	200.00	Long	Entry	196.00			
3-30	208.40		Trade out		2,000		
3-30	208.40		Completed			(875)	(725)
4-02	208.40	Long	Entry	204.40			
6-29	218.60		Trade out		2,450		
6-29	218.60		Completed			(2,550)	(100)
7-02	218.60	Long	Entry	214.60			
9-14	221.00	Short	Continued	214.60			
9-28	223.20		Trade out		1,050		
9-28	223.20		Completed			(1,150)	(100)
10-01	223.20	Short	No entry				
11-19	222.20	Long	Entry	218.20			
11-26	218.70	Short	Continued	218.20			
11-29	221.31	Long	Continued	218.20			
12-31	224.60		Trade out		500		
12-31	224.60		Completed			(350)	150
1980							
1-02	224.60	Long	Entry	220.60			
3-06	227.00	Short	No exit	220.60			
3-31	222.10		Trade out		(725)		
3-31	222.10		Completed			625	(100)
4-01	222.10	Short	No entry				
4-21	230.60	Long	Entry	226.60			

TABLE 9.1. (Continued)

Date	Exposure Price	Model Direction	Hedge Action	Risk Stop	Trade Gain/Loss (+ Commission)	Market Move	Hedge Net
6-30	240.40		Trade out		2,350		
6-30	240.40		Completed			(4,575)	(2,125)
7-01	240.40	Long	Entry	236.40			
9-30	248.20		Trade out		1,850		
9-30	248.20		Completed			(1,950)	(100)
10-01	248.20	Long	Entry	244.20			
11-19	248.40	Short	No exit	244.20			
12-24	251.20	Long	Continued	247.20			
12-31	252.40		Trade out		950		
12-31	252.40		Completed			(1,050)	(100)
1981							
1-02	241.50	Long	Entry	237.50			
1-30	238.60	Short	No exit	237.50			
1-30	236.30		Out on risk stop		(1,400)		
3-31	221.55		Completed			4,987	3,587
4-01	221.55	Short	No entry				
6-30	187.95		Completed			8,400	8,400
7-01	187.95	Short	No entry				
9-30	171.95		Completed			4,000	4,000
10-01	171.95	Short	No entry				
10-08	180.05	Long	Entry	176.05			
10-15	174.80	Short	Exit		(1,412)		
10-30	177.70	Long	Entry	173.70			
12-31	181.90		Trade out		950		
12-31	181.90		Completed			(2,488)	(2,950)
1982							
1-04	181.90	Long	Entry	177.90			
1-13	177.74	Short	No exit	177.90			
1-13	177.00		Out on risk stop		(1,325)		
3-31	169.35		Completed			3,137	1,812
4-01	169.35	Short	No entry				
5-07	173.30	Long	Entry	169.30			
5-19	170.00	Short	No exit	169.30			
5-19	169.30		Out on risk stop		(1,100)		
6-30	164.10		Completed			1,312	212
7-01	164.10	Short	No entry				
8-24	166.25	Long	Entry	162.25			
8-27	163.25	Short	No exit	162.25			

TABLE 9.1. (Continued)

Date	Exposure Price	Model Direction	Hedge Action	Risk Stop	Trade Gain/Loss (+ Commission)	Market Move	Hedge Net
8-27	162.25		Out on risk stop		(1,100)		
9-30	158.80		Completed			1,325	225
10-01	158.80	Short	No entry				
12-31	151.40		Completed			1,850	1,850
1983							
1-03	162.40	Short	No entry				
3-31	148.25		Completed			3,537	3,537
4-04	148.25	Short	No entry				
4-12	153.15	Long	Entry	149.15			
6-14	152.89	Short	No exit	149.15			
6-24	155.20	Long	Continued	151.20			
6-27	153.37	Short	Continued				
6-30	153.20		Trade out		(112)		
6-30	153.20		Completed			(1,238)	(1,350)
7-01	153.20	Short	No entry				
9-30	149.60		Completed			900	900
10-03	149.60	Short	No entry				
10-07	152.05	Long	Entry	148.05			
10-12	150.15	Short	No exit	148.05			
11-18	146.90		Out on risk stop		(1,388)		
12-30	146.15		Completed			862	(526)
1984							
1-03	146.15	Short	No entry				
2-15	144.44	Long	Entry	140.44			
3-30	144.30		Trade out		(135)		
3-30	144.30		Completed			463	323
4-02	144.30	Long	Entry	140.30			
4-05	142.62	Short	No exit	140.30			
4-27	140.15		Out on risk stop		(1,138)		
6-29	135.30		Completed			2,250	1,112
7-02	135.30	Short	No entry				
9-28	121.90		Completed			3,350	3,350
10-01	121.90	Short	No entry				
11-07	125.91	Long	Entry	121.91			
11-19	122.91	Short	No exit	121.91			
11-20	121.89		Out on risk stop		(1,105)		
12-31	113.34		Completed			2,140	1,035

TABLE 9.1. (*Continued*)

Date	Exposure Price	Model Direction	Hedge Action	Risk Stop	Trade Gain/Loss (+ Commission)	Market Move	Hedge Net
1985							
1-02	113.34	Short	No entry				
3-19	111.93	Long	Entry	107.93			
3-29	122.08		Trade out		2,438		
3-29	122.08		Completed			(2,185)	300
4-02	122.08	Long	Entry	118.08			
6-30	129.73		Trade out		1,813	(1,913)	(100)
7-01	129.73	Long	Entry	125.73			
9-06	132.78	Short	No exit	125.73			
9-30	139.53		Trade out		2,350		
9-30	139.53		Completed			(2,450)	(100)
10-01	139.53	Long	Entry	135.53			
12-31	146.03		Trade out		1,525		
12-31	146.03		Completed			(1,625)	(100)
TOTAL							$26,092

were losers, and 13 were fully hedged with only 1 trade. The largest loser occurred during the fourth quarter of 1981 when there were two trades and the model effectively missed the market move. This losing quarter cost the hedger $2,950 on an exposure of $42,987, or about 7 percent of the hedge. The average annual gain from selectively hedging came out to $2,609. The largest quarterly gain was $8,400.

We now turn to the short hedge for the same period (Table 9.2). We use the same rules (1–5) except that *long* now becomes *short*. For the short hedger; 17 periods were winners, 13 were fully hedged with one trade, and 10 were losers. The largest loser was $1,312. The largest winner was $3,950. The average annual gain totaled $1,690.

Combining both long and short hedges gives 37 winners, 17 losers, and 26 fully hedged with only 1 trade. The total number of trades numbered 72, or less than 1 per period. These represented a commission overhead cost of $7,200. Rarely did any three-month period have more than one trade. We conclude that selectively hedging the British pound would have been profitable as a way to

TABLE 9.2. QUARTERLY SHORT HEDGER STUDY OF THE BRITISH POUND OVER THE 1976–1985 PERIOD, USING THE OPTIMIZED KELTNER MODEL FOR TIMING.

Date	Exposure Price	Model Direction	Hedge Action	Risk Stop	Trade Gain/Loss (+ Commission)	Market Move	Hedge Net
1976							
1-02	200.40	Short	Entry	204.40			
1-05	201.40	Long	No exit	204.40			
3-05	196.80	Short	Continued	200.80			
3-31	191.70		Trade Out		2,075		
3-31	191.70		Completed			(2,175)	(100)
4-01	191.70	Short	Entry	195.70			
6-30	179.40		Trade out		2,975		
6-30	179.40		Completed			(3,075)	(100)
7-01	179.40	Short	Entry	183.40			
7-28	180.60	Long	No exit	183.40			
9-08	178.80	Short	Continued	182.80			
9-30	169.20		Trade out		2,475		
9-30	169.10		Completed			(2,575)	(100)
10-01	169.10	Short	Entry	173.10			
11-18	173.20	Long	No exit	173.10			
11-18	174.00		Out on risk stop		(1,125)		
11-22	171.30	Short	Entry	175.30			
11-23	172.90	Long	No exit	175.30			
11-24	170.90	Short	Continued	174.90			
12-02	172.50	Long	No exit	174.90			
12-22	175.40		Out on risk stop		(1,225)		
12-30	176.70		Completed			1,900	(650)
1977							
1-03	170.10	Long	No entry				
3-31	178.40		Completed			2,075	2,075
4-01	178.40	Long	No entry				
5-31	177.10	Short	Entry	181.10			
6-02	178.00	Long	No exit	181.10			
6-30	179.50		Trade out		(600)		
6-30	179.50		Completed			275	(425)
7-01	179.50	Long	No entry				
9-30	184.40		Completed			1,225	1,225
10-03	184.40	Long	No entry				
12-30	200.20		Completed			3,950	3,950
1978							
1-03	200.20	Long	No entry				
3-10	198.50	Short	Entry	202.50			

178

TABLE 9.2. (Continued)

Date	Exposure Price	Model Direction	Hedge Action	Risk Stop	Trade Gain/Loss (+ Commission)	Market Move	Hedge Net
3-31	194.60		Trade out		875		
3-31	194.60		Completed			(1,400)	(525)
4-03	194.60	Short	Entry	198.60			
6-21	193.70	Long	No exit	198.60			
6-30	194.10		Trade out		25		
6-30	194.10		Completed			(125)	(100)
7-03	194.10	Long	No entry				
9-29	206.50		Completed			3,100	3,100
10-02	206.50	Long	No entry				
11-16	205.80	Short	Entry	209.80			
12-11	208.30	Long	No exit	209.80			
12-18	211.10		Out on risk stop		(1,425)		
12-29	215.70		Completed			2,300	875
1979							
1-02	204.90	Long	No entry				
2-01	197.90	Short	Entry	201.90			
2-06	200.00	Long	No exit	201.90			
2-23	202.50		Out on risk stop		(1,250)		
3-30	208.40		Completed			875	(375)
4-02	208.40	Long	No entry				
6-29	218.60		Completed			2,550	2,550
7-02	218.60	Long	No entry				
9-14	221.00	Short	Entry	225.00			
9-28	223.20		Trade out		(650)		
9-28	223.20		Completed			1,150	500
10-01	223.20	Short	Entry	227.20			
11-19	222.20	Long	No exit	227.20			
11-26	218.70	Short	Continued	222.70			
11-29	221.30	Long	Continued	222.70			
12-27	225.50		Out on risk stop		(675)		
12-31	224.60		Completed			350	(325)
1980							
1-02	224.60	Long	No entry				
3-06	227.00	Short	Entry	231.00			
3-31	222.10		Trade out		1,225		
3-31	222.10		Completed			(625)	600
4-01	222.10	Short	Entry	226.10			
4-10	226.10		Out on risk stop		(1,175)		

TABLE 9.2. (*Continued*)

Date	Exposure Price	Model Direction	Hedge Action	Risk Stop	Trade Gain/Loss (+ Commission)	Market Move	Hedge Net
4-21	230.60	Long	No entry				
6-30	240.40		Completed			4,575	3,400
7-01	240.40	Long	No entry				
9-30	248.20		Completed			1,950	1,950
10-01	248.20	Long	No entry				
11-19	248.40	Short	Entry	252.40			
12-24	251.20	Long	Continued	252.40			
12-31	252.40		Trade out		(1,100)		
12-31	252.40		Completed			1,050	(50)
1981							
1-02	241.50	Long	No entry				
1-30	238.60	Short	Entry	242.60			
3-31	221.55		Trade out		4,262		
3-31	221.55		Completed			(4,987)	(725)
4-01	221.55	Short	Entry	225.55			
6-30	187.95		Trade out		8,300		
6-30	187.95		Completed			(8,400)	(100)
7-01	187.95	Short	Entry	191.95			
9-30	171.95		Trade out		3,900		
9-30	171.95		Completed			(4,000)	(100)
10-01	171.95	Short	Entry	175.95			
10-05	176.40		Out on risk stop		(1,212)		
10-08	180.05	Long	No entry				
10-15	174.80	Short	Entry	178.80			
10-30	177.70	Long	No exit	178.80			
10-30	178.80		Out on risk stop		(1,100)		
12-31	181.90		Completed			2,488	176
1982							
1-04	181.90	Long	No Entry				
1-13	177.74	Short	Entry	181.74			
3-31	169.35		Trade out		1,997		
3-31	169.35		Completed			(3,137)	(1,140)
4-01	169.35	Short	Entry	173.35			
5-07	173.30	Long	No exit	173.35			
5-07	174.45		Out on risk stop		(1,375)		
5-19	170.00	Short	Entry	174.00			
6-30	164.10		Trade out		1,375		
6-30	164.10		Completed			(1,312)	(1,312)

TABLE 9.2. (*Continued*)

Date	Exposure Price	Model Direction	Hedge Action	Risk Stop	Trade Gain/Loss (+ Commission)	Market Move	Hedge Net
7-01	164.10	Short	Entry	168.10			
8-24	166.25	Long	No exit	168.10			
8-27	163.25	Short	Continued	167.25			
9-30	158.80		Trade out		1,325		
9-30	158.80		Completed			(1,325)	(100)
10-01	158.80	Short	Entry	162.80			
12-31	151.40		Trade out		1,750		
12-31	151.40		Completed			(1,850)	(100)
1983							
1-03	162.40	Short	Entry	166.40			
3-31	148.25		Trade out		3,457		
3-31	148.25		Completed			(3,537)	(100)
4-04	148.25	Short	Entry	152.25			
4-11	152.80		Out on risk stop		(1,137)		
4-12	153.15	Long	No entry				
6-14	152.89	Short	Entry	156.89			
6-24	155.20	Long	No exit	156.89			
6-27	153.37	Short	Continued	156.89			
6-30	153.20		Trade out		(175)		
6-30	153.20		Completed			1,238	(74)
7-01	153.20	Short	Entry	157.20			
9-30	149.60		Trade out		800		
9-30	149.60		Completed			(900)	(100)
10-03	149.60	Short	Entry	153.60			
10-07	152.05	Long	No exit	153.60			
10-12	150.15	Short	Continued	153.60			
12-30	146.15		Trade out		762		
12-30	146.15		Completed			(862)	(100)
1984							
1-03	146.15	Short	Entry	150.15			
2-15	144.44	Long	No exit	150.15			
3-30	144.30		Trade out		363		
3-30	144.30		Completed			(463)	(100)
4-02	144.30	Long	No entry				
4-05	142.62	Short	Entry	146.62			
6-29	135.20		Trade out		1,730		
6-29	135.30		Completed			(2,250)	(520)
7-02	135.30	Short	Entry	139.30			
9-28	121.90		Trade out		3,250		
9-28	121.90		Completed			(3,350)	(100)

TABLE 9.2.   (*Continued*)

Date	Exposure Price	Model Direction	Hedge Action	Risk Stop	Trade Gain/Loss (+ Commission)	Market Move	Hedge Net
10-01	121.90	Short	Entry	125.90			
11-07	125.91	Long	Exit		(1,100)		
11-19	122.91	Short	Entry	126.91			
12-31	113.34		Trade out		2,293		
12-31	113.34		Completed			(2,140)	(947)
1985							
1-02	113.34	Short	Entry	117.34			
3-19	111.93	Long	No exit				
3-27	121.33		Out on risk stop		(2,098)		
3-29	122.08		Completed			2,185	87
4-02	122.08	Long	No entry				
6-69	129.73		Completed			1,913	1,913
7-01	129.73	Long	No entry				
9-06	132.78	Short	Entry	136.78			
9-20	136.83	Long	Exit		(1,300)		
9-30	139.53		Completed			2,450	1,250
10-01	139.53	Long	No entry				
12-31	146.03		Completed			1,625	1,625
TOTAL							$16,908

insure against adverse market moves. The price of insurance is, in the long run, free.

In Table 9.3 we present a summary of the quarterly long and short hedger studies for comparison with the hedge-and-hold. We assume no commission costs for the hedge-and-hold and deduct $100 commission per trade for the selective hedge. Note that the hedge-and-hold hedger would have netted zero gain and zero loss in every hedge period (ignoring basis change).

Once again, had both the long and short hedgers used the hedge-and-hold rather than the selective hedge as in Table 9.3, they would have netted zero gain and zero loss in every hedge period (ignoring basis change). On the contrary, selective hedgers showed consistent gains (in addition to being fully hedged), with only a scattering of minor losses.

TABLE 9.3. LONG- AND SHORT-HEDGE PERFORMANCE SUMMARY FOR THE BRITISH POUND, 1976–1985, USING THE OPTIMIZED 68-DAY MOVING AVERAGE KELTNER MODEL

Hedge Period	Long Hedger		Short Hedger	
	Period Net	Yearly Net	Period Net	Yearly Net
3-31-76	1,025		0	
6-30-76	3,175		0	
9-30-76	1,300		0	
12-30-76	(925)	4,575	(550)	(550)
3-31-77	0		2,175	
6-30-77	0		(325)	
9-30-77	0		1,325	
12-30-77	0	0	4,050	7,225
3-31-78	(25)		(425)	
6-30-78	225		0	
9-29-78	0		3,200	
12-27-78	200	400	975	3,750
3-30-79	(625)		(275)	
6-30-79	0		2,650	
9-28-79	0		600	
12-31-79	250	(375)	(225)	2,750
3-31-80	0		700	
6-30-80	(2,025)		3,500	
9-30-80	0		2,050	
12-31-80	0	(2,025)	50	6,300
3-31-81	3,687		(625)	
6-30-81	8,500		0	
9-30-81	4,100		0	
12-31-81	(2,850)	13,437	276	(349)
3-31-82	1,912		(1,040)	
6-30-82	312		(1,212)	
9-30-82	325		0	
12-31-82	1,950	4,499	0	(2,252)
3-31-83	3637		0	
6-30-83	(1,250)		(74)	
9-30-83	1,000		0	
12-30-83	(426)	2,961	0	(74)

TABLE 9.3.   (Continued)

Hedge Period	Long Hedger		Short Hedger	
	Period Net	Yearly Net	Period Net	Yearly Net
3-30-84	423		0	
6-29-84	1,212		(420)	
9-28-84	3,450		0	
12-31-84	1,135	6,220	(847)	(1,267)
3-29-85	400		187	
6-29-85	0		2,013	
9-30-85	0		1,350	
12-31-85	0	400	1,725	5,275
TOTAL		30,092		20,808

Note: Hedges are broken down into three-month hedge periods. Results above are in comparison to the hedge-and-hold, therefore a $100 commission is deducted for each period.

Hedging with the 10-Day Keltner Trading Model

The previous hedging study used the optimized 68-day Keltner trading model as the hedging guide, and the model performed consistently in the hedger's favor. As noted earlier, the optimized model was chosen for the longer term quarterly study primarily because it generates fewer trades and therefore makes for easier illustration. It is also the way a real-life hedger would behave. The authors feel that to some, this study may seem somewhat incomplete unless the father model, the standard 10-day Keltner, is also shown to be useful as a selective hedging guide under the same conditions. A smaller study of the British pound, using the standard Keltner and assuming the same conditions (1–5) as with the longer-term study, is therefore included for completeness. Table 9.4 covers the 1981 through 1983 period for a long hedger, again using Continua data for the input. This three-year period demonstrates the model's performance over the two fundamental market characteristics—trending and nontrending. From January 1981 through March 1982 the pound was in the midst of a strong downtrend, falling from $2.40 to around $1.60. Then from April 1982

TABLE 9.4. QUARTERLY LONG HEDGER STUDY OF THE BRITISH POUND OVER THE 1981–1983 PERIOD, USING THE STANDARD (10-DAY) KELTNER MODEL FOR TIMING

Date	Exposure Price	Model Direction	Hedge Action	Risk Stop	Trade Gain/Loss (+ Commission)	Market Move	Hedge Net
1981							
1-02	241.50	Long	Entry	237.50			
1-15	240.26	Short	No exit	237.50			
1-19	243.15	Long	Continued	239.15			
1-29	240.61	Short	Continued	239.15			
1-30	236.30		Out on risk stop		(1,400)		
3-10	221.83	Long	Entry	217.83			
3-26	221.59	Short	No exit	217.83			
3-31	221.55		Trade out		(170)		
3-31	221.55		Completed			4,987	3,417
4-01	221.55	Short	No entry				
6-15	195.19	Long	Entry	191.19			
6-25	192.10	Short	No exit	191.19			
6-25	190.20		Out on risk stop		(1,347)		
6-30	187.95		Completed			8,400	7,053
7-01	187.95	Short	No entry				
8-12	177.18	Long	Entry	173.18			
9-01	176.39	Short	No exit	173.18			
9-08	171.90		Out on risk stop		(1,420)		
9-16	176.92	Long	Entry	172.92			
9-24	170.35	Short	Exit		(1,643)		
9-30	171.95		Completed			4,000	937
10-01	171.95	Short	No entry				
10-05	175.05	Long	Entry	171.05			
10-15	175.25	Short	No exit	171.05			
10-29	175.13	Long	Continued	171.13			
12-08	182.47	Short	Continued	171.13			
12-31	181.90		Trade out		1,612		
12-31	181.90		Completed			(2,488)	(875)
1982							
1-04	181.90	Long	Entry	177.90			
1-13	177.75	Short	No exit	177.90			
1-13	177.00		Out on risk stop		(1,325)		
3-31	169.35		Completed			3,137	1,812
4-01	169.35	Short	No entry				
4-21	168.15	Long	Entry	164.15			
5-17	171.66	Short	No exit	164.15			

185

TABLE 9.4. (Continued)

Date	Exposure Price	Model Direction	Hedge Action	Risk Stop	Trade Gain/Loss (+ Commission)	Market Move	Hedge Net
6-30	164.10		Trade out		(1,012)		
6-30	164.10		Completed			1,312	200
7-01	164.10	Short	No entry				
7-16	163.97	Long	Entry	159.97			
7-28	162.97	Short	No exit	159.97			
8-06	159.90		Out on risk stop		(1,117)		
8-18	162.60	Long	Entry	158.60			
8-30	161.34	Short	No exit	158.60			
9-27	158.30		Out on risk stop		(1,175)		
9-30	158.80		Completed			1,325	(967)
10-01	158.80	Short	No entry				
10-07	159.79	Long	Entry	155.79			
10-19	158.74	Short	No exit	155.79			
11-04	155.70		Out on risk stop		(1,122)		
11-30	150.42	Long	Entry	146.42			
12-08	148.68	Short	No exit	146.42			
12-31	151.40		Trade out		145		
12-31	151.40		Completed			1,850	873
1983							
1-03	162.40	Long	Entry	158.40			
1-06	159.55	Short	No exit	158.40			
1-10	157.00		Out on risk stop		(1,450)		
2-08	153.10	Long	Entry	149.10			
2-22	151.30	Short	No exit	149.10			
3-08	148.75		Out on risk stop		(1,087)		
3-14	151.00	Long	Entry	147.00			
3-18	148.80	Short	No exit	147.00			
3-21	147.00		Out on risk stop		(1,100)		
3-31	148.25		Completed			3,537	(100)
4-04	148.25	Long	Entry	144.25			
5-10	155.95	Short	No exit	144.25			
5-23	156.84	Long	Continued	152.84			
6-03	155.90	Short	Continued	152.84			
6-24	155.20	Long	Continued	152.84			
6-27	153.37	Short	Continued	152.84			
6-30	153.20		Trade out		1,138		
6-30	153.20		Completed			(1,238)	(100)

TABLE 9.4. (*Continued*)

Date	Exposure Price	Model Direction	Hedge Action	Risk Stop	Trade Gain/Loss (+ Commission)	Market Move	Hedge Net
7-01	153.20	Long	Entry	149.20			
7-14	153.10	Short	No exit	149.20			
7-27	153.52	Long	Continued	149.52			
7-29	152.14	Short	Continued	149.52			
8-10	148.70		Out on risk stop		(1,225)		
8-16	150.70	Long	Entry	146.70			
8-25	150.40	Short	No exit	146.70			
9-12	150.80	Long	Continued	146.80			
9-14	149.17	Short	Continued	146.80			
9-16	150.51	Long	Continued	146.80			
9-29	149.70	Short	Continued	146.80			
9-30	149.60		Trade out		(375)		
9-30	149.60		Completed			900	(600)
10-03	149.60	Short	No entry				
10-06	150.39	Long	Entry	146.39			
10-27	149.20	Short	No exit	146.39			
11-28	145.90		Out on risk stop		(1,222)		
12-30	146.15		Completed			862	(360)

through December 1983 the pound was virtually trendless, hovering around $1.50 for the entire period. The standard Keltner is shown to perform admirably over both strongly trending and tougher, flat markets.

A summary of the quarterly long hedger positions for comparison with the hedge-and-hold is provided in Table 9.5. Note that the hedge-and-hold hedger would have netted zero gain and zero loss in every period (omitting basis change).

Based on the results in Table 9.5, the standard Keltner model also appears to be useful as a selective hedging guide. Over the 12-quarter period there were 6 winning quarters, 4 losers, and 2 where the hedger was covered with only 1 trade. The total gain was $12,816, or a quarterly average of $1,068. Thus using this basic model the hedger was fully hedged during two-thirds of the quarters while averaging 8.5 percent return annually. Over the same period the optimized model produced 9 winning quarters, 3 losers

TABLE 9.5.   LONG HEDGE PERFORMANCE SUMMARY FOR THE
BRITISH POUND, 1981–1983, USING THE STANDARD (10-DAY)
KELTNER MOVING AVERAGE TRADING MODEL

	Long Hedger	
Hedge Period	Period Net	Yearly Net
3-31-81	3,517	
6-30-81	7,153	
9-30-81	1,363	
12-31-81	(775)	11,258
3-31-82	1,912	
6-30-82	300	
9-30-82	(867)	
12-31-82	973	2,318
3-31-83	0	
6-30-83	0	
9-30-83	(500)	
12-30-83	(260)	(760)
Total		12,816

Note: Hedges are broken into three-month hedge periods and results are shown in comparison to the hedge-and-hold ($100 commission is deducted for each period).

and netted $20,897, or $1,741 per quarter. The *optimized* hedger was fully hedged over 75 percent of the quarters while returning nearly 15 percent per year. While the optimized model was nearly twice as profitable, it also embodied greater risk. The average losing trade for the standard was $700, compared to $1,600 for the optimized.

Comparing the two models trade-by-trade (see Tables 9.1 and 9.5), the standard Keltner trades nearly three times as often as the optimized, as is to be expected. Over the three-year period studied, the standard recommended 26 trades (long trades only) versus 8 for the optimized. However, note that because the hedger assumes a $1,000 risk margin and places trading stops accordingly (rule 5), the hedger using the standard model reduced the number of trades to 19.

SELECTIVELY HEDGING CONTINGENT EXPOSURES

A contingent exposure is one that depends on a future transaction that may or may not occur. Such situations were mentioned briefly in Chapters 2 and 3. These are special exposures that need to be covered in the present in the event that they materialize in the future. As an example, company A in the U.S. competes with company B in West Germany for precision pipe sales to company C in a third country. As the dollar strengthens relative to the deutsche mark, it becomes increasingly difficult for A to meet B's prices. A large percentage drop in the deutsche mark (e.g., over 30 percent in 1984), would put A totally out of contention. The real problem faced by A is not one of remaining competitive, but rather *preparing* to remain competitive (another problem is doing it at a reasonable cost). In Chapter 3 we introduced options as one practical way to manage contingent risk. Another possible solution to A's dilemma is a hedge that is employed only as needed, a so-called selective contingent hedge. It is the aim of this section to examine a selective hedge using futures that offer protection under many potential conditions.

If company A had known in advance that the deutsche mark would fall relative to the dollar, a simple forward contract could have been placed for the appropriate time period. Unfortunately, it is very difficult to know currency directions in advance. At the beginning of 1984, the U.S. economic picture led most economists to predict a falling dollar. The pundits were wrong and had A remained unhedged (the proper strategy for a rising mark), they would have become noncompetitive, as previously noted. If, on the other hand, the experts had predicted a strengthening dollar, and A hedged; a subsequent weakening dollar would have netted A a real loss. This loss would have arisen whether any biddable jobs arose or not. This uncertainty in market direction and the eventuation of biddable jobs militates against any standard hedge-and-hold strategy. A specialized selective hedge offers hope of both keeping A competitive while keeping the risk of market loss down.

Recall that the primary characteristic of the selective hedge is its aim to be hedged only when the market is moving against the position. A only needs to be hedged if the deutsche mark falls and it is believed that biddable jobs are in the offing. A practical problem for A is determination of the appropriate time-frame for the bidding analysis. If too short, the average market move is not completed within the bid-time. If too long, smoothing effects of up and down moves may negate the value of hedging.

Clearly, A needs to have an idea of the structure of the deutsche mark market behavior. In Chapter 8 hedging on the basis of trading models was discussed and illustrated. That technique could be followed here, but it may be more instructive to utilize an index instead. The index is more flexible, so that market movement, by itself, is the element studied. There are numerous indexes in the literature. The one used here is the CISCO Consensus Moving Average Index.[1] Based on a number of moving averages of differing length, the index goes from 1, most bearish, to most bullish at 99. From the general index, the deutsche mark index is developed by application of two hedging rules:

1. A long position is assumed when the index passes upward through the value of 68 and is held until the decline moves down through 50.

2. A short position is initiated when the index goes down through 32 and is maintained until the index recovers to 50.

The deutsche mark index does not have to be in the market at all times, but in fact, usually is. Of course, A would only want to be hedged short; their hedge would be employed only about half the time.

Table 9.6 shows how the deutsche mark index behaved over the 1979 through 1985 period.

Collecting the data of Table 9.6 gives Table 9.7. Referring to Tables 9.6 and 9.7, there were a total of 27 wins and 32 losses over the 7 years of the study. The wins totaled 676.7 points (at $125 per point), while the losses cost only 195.2 points. Seventy-eight percent of the trading was contained in the wins. The average win was 25 points, over 4 times the average loss of 6 points. Most losses were small, with the largest, 20.5 points, occurring at the devaluation of September 23, 1985. For the seven years of the study the in-

TABLE 9.6.   DEUTSCHE MARK INDEX SIGNAL RESULTS USING THE
CISCO CONTINUA™ DATA FOR THE PERIOD 1978–1985

Time Period	Direction	Gain/Loss	Days
1978			
12-21 1-23-79	L	− 0.9	33
1979			
1-26 . . . . 2- 7	S	− 5.8	14
2- 8 6-15	S	22.1	127
6-15 7-31	L	11.1	46
8- 8 8-14	L	− 0.9	6
8-14 8-30	S	− 0.8	16
9- 4 . . . . 9- 5	S	− 2.1	1
9- 6 10-16	L	0.2	40
10-23 . . . . 11- 2	S	− 3.9	10
11- 9 11-14	S	− 6.2	5
11-16 1-15-80	L	6.8	60
1980			
1-18 4-17	S	42.7	90
4-22 4-23	S	− 10.8	1
4-24 7-29	L	8.9	96
7-30 . . . . 9- 2	S	− 2.6	34
9-16 3-18-81	S	40.5	183
1981			
3-18 3-26	L	− 19.6	8
3-26 3-30	S	− 11.5	4
4- 2 8-31	S	73.0	151
9- 2 10-26	L	16.2	54
10-30 11-16	L	− 7.2	16
11-19 11-27	S	− 10.1	8
11-27 . . . . 12- 1	L	− 4.9	4
12- 2 . . . . 12- 3	L	− 3.5	1
12- 7 12-31	S	0.0	24
1982			
7-28 . . . . 8- 2	S	− 6.0	5
8- 4 8-20	S	− 3.8	16
8-23 8-27	L	− 6.1	4
8-27 10-11	S	1.3	45
10-12 11-23	S	8.3	42
11-24 1-19-83	L	24.9	55

TABLE 9.6.   (*Continued*)

Time Period	Direction	Gain/Loss	Days
1983			
1-19 2-14	S	−4.1	26
2-22 . . . . 3- 4	S	−7.6	10
3- 4 3-22	L	−4.4	18
3-23 . . . . 4- 5	S	−1.2	13
4- 8 9-19	S	43.5	164
9-23 10-31	L	−0.7	38
11- 1 . . . . 2- 2-84	L	17.3	93
1984			
2- 2 . . . . 4- 3	L	15.5	61
4- 9 . . . . 6- 1	S	10.3	53
6-14 10-24	S	45.9	132
10-29 10-31	S	−6.2	2
11- 1 11-20	L	−3.1	19
11-26 3-19-85	S	55.3	113
1985			
3-21 . . . . 5- 2	L	1.8	42
5- 3 . . . . 5- 9	S	−11.1	6
5-13 5-24	L	−4.1	11
5-28 5-29	S	−4.8	1
5-31 . . . . 6- 7	L	−4.6	8
6-17 6-24	L	−0.6	7
6-26 . . . . 9- 3	L	19.8	69
9- 3 . . . . 9-23 *	S	−20.5	20
9-23 12-31	L	35.6	99

Note: The Time Period column lists the entry date and the exit date. Direction is the direction of the recommendation, L for long, or upward trending price, S for short, or downward price. The gain/loss column gives the theoretical close-to-close change for the period covered. A gain/loss value of 1.0 represents a move of $125 for one futures contract. Last, the days column is the number of days the recommendation was held. Losing recommendations are identified by minus signs. The * on 9-23-85 marks the date of major central bank intervention to devalue the U.S. dollar.

dex was in the market 2501 days, or approximately 97 percent of the time. Winning recommendations occupied 2105 days, losing covered just 396. Thus 84 percent of the time the index was on the correct side of the market. The average recommendation covered 42 days.

TABLE 9.7.   ANNUAL VALUES COLLECTED FROM TABLE 9.6

		Gain/Loss	Days
1979	3 Wins	73.4	213
	7 Losses	− 20.6	85
	1 Tie	0.0	24
1980	4 Wins	118.2	429
	2 Losses	− 13.4	35
1981	4 Wins	133.2	205
	5 Losses	− 53.3	65
1982	6 Wins	60.7	332
	4 Losses	− 31.4	30
1983	1 Win	43.5	164
	5 Losses	− 18.0	105
1984	5 Wins	144.3	552
	2 Losses	− 9.2	21
1985	4 Wins	103.4	210
	7 Losses	− 49.2	55

Note: The gain/loss column is now the totals for the year. Days is totals as well.

The index statistics can be used by company A to help determine the proper time frame for hedging. If the inherent market scale is approximately a month and a half, the companies' time scale should at least be several times that. Six months would cover four average market moves, which would normally be adequate. Also, six months could well be an appropriate time scale for estimating the potential occurrence of bidding opportunities. If the company can utilize a longer time frame—say nine months or a year—so much the better. The longer the time for the selective hedge, the more likely that the average statistics of win/lose will prevail.

The protection of contingent exposure is a prime use for the selective hedge and illustrates several of the real world problems multinational marketers face. The definition of exposure is complicated due to both differential currency rate movements and an intangible part based on the managements' perceived need to remain competitive. Time frames for action are a dynamic function of the currency market (as illustrated by the index) and the market environment for the companies' products. Management alone is in a position to evaluate their marketplace. Generally, only probabilities are available. It is only after tying the pieces together and arriving at a most likely scenario that a hedge strategy can be developed. Ultimately, the decision to hedge or not to hedge and, if so, how much, resides with management. These important and sometimes critical decisions should not be left to bankers or brokers. Once management is clear on its course of action, the technical tools such as the index model, or futures or options trading models, can be followed for timing.

APPLYING TIMING TO INTERNAL METHODS

In Chapter 8 and the earlier sections of this chapter we demonstrated the effectiveness of using a timing model to guide the placement of a hedge. Thus far, our timing analysis has focused on its application to "canned" external methods such as forward and futures contracts. But a hedge is a hedge is a hedge. And virtually any hedge, internal or external, can benefit from timing. In this section we study the effect of timing on the internal methods.

Exchange rate expectations played a central role in many of the internal techniques of Chapter 3. Such forecasts helped to determine whether to borrow or lend locally, lead or lag, and so forth. Regardless of the forecast's origin, that is, one's banker, treasury department, or some econometric model, eventually the question "When do I place the hedge?" must be answered. We will demonstrate that technical timing is a valuable aid in timing payments internally, just as it was for the external hedge. In the simple case that follows, such timing nets nearly 14 percent per annum, a surprisingly large return for an unsophisticated model.

Timing Lead/Lag Decisions

By definition, companies that support lead/lag policies (see Chapter 3) are prime candidates for timing of some kind. Take, for instance, a U.S. firm with payables in British pounds. If the pound is expected to depreciate during the payment period, common sense says lag if possible. Conversely, if a stronger pound is anticipated the firm should consider paying immediately (leading). Leading or lagging an individual payment is a one-time decision. But the critical question still remains: When? The decision-making process for lead/lag situations is similar to that of the modified hedge-and-hold hedger (M H/H; see Chapter 7). Recall that the M H/H approach uses timing from a model for the initial placement of the hedge. The hedge then remains in place for the duration of the exposure period. This is practically identical with one-time lead/lag decisions.

Earlier, in this chapter we presented a selective hedge study, by quarter, of the British pound over the 1976 through 1985 period. In this section, we will take the same trading data from Tables 9.1 and 9.2 and apply it to quarterly lead/lag decisions, except that we use a M H/H rather than a selective hedge approach. For illustrative purposes we will create arbitrary lead/lag situations at the start of each quarter. Thus every three months the hedger must decide whether to cover the new 90-day payables immediately, at some time during the period, or at the period's end. The hedge conditions 1 through 5 (from an earlier section) are adapted to reflect the M H/H lead/lag perspective:

1. The hedger contracts a debt denominated in pounds. Thus if pounds gain against the dollar this hedger will lose.

2. The debt is contracted as of the first day of the quarter, with a due date of the last day of the quarter.

3. For consistency we will assume the size of the debt to be BP 25,000, or equal to one futures contract.

4. An M H/H hedge is elected.

5. The hedger will use the model for entry only. Once the decision to lead or lag is made, it is held for the duration of the quarter.

As before, we use the Continua data for the input and the 68-day Keltner for timing. The lead/lag period is a calendar quarter, with the starting exposure price as the close of the day prior to the quarter start. The ending point is the close on the last day of the quarter.

Of course, the time period chosen is arbitrary, but the very arbitrariness ensures a fair test. The actual usage would be for any needed period.

To take full advantage of the model's signals, we will use an intercompany lead/lag situation for our example (see Chapter 3). We assume that intercompany payables (both parent to subsidiary and subsidiary to parent) are denominated in pounds. Our simple intercompany scenario is as follows:

1. The lead/lag decisions involve a U.S. parent and its British subsidiary.
2. All decisions are handed down from the parent.
3. The parent's lead/lag policy when the model is short (the pount is expected to weaken):
   a. The U.S. parent lags payment to the British subsidiary.
   b. The subsidiary leads payment to the parent.
4. The parent's lead/lag policy when the model is long (the pound is expected to strengthen):
   a. The parent leads payment to the subsidiary.
   b. The subsidiary lags payment to the parent.

If the trading model is already in the market long at the start of the quarter the parent immediately pays the debt to the subsidiary. Meanwhile, the subsidiary lags payments to the parent. If during the same quarter the model reverses to short the subsidiary stops lagging and pays the debt. If the model is short at the start of the period the parent lags payment to the subsidiary and instructs the subsidiary to lead (pay) British payables due to the parent. This continues until the model returns long or the close of the last day, whichever occurs first. In Table 9.8 we list the model's signals (from Tables 9.1 and 9.2), action taken by the parent and the subsidiary, and lead/lag results. Of the 40 quarters, in 24 (or 60 percent) the hedger profited from the lead/lag decision. Sixteen of the quarters produced a net loss. The cumulative gain over the 10-year period was $62,000 on a continuous exposure valued at roughly $45,000 (BP 25,000 * $1.80).

TABLE 9.8.   THE RESULTS OF LEAD/LAG DECISIONS BASED ON THE
KELTNER TIMING MODEL OVER 1976–1985

Date	Price	Model Direction	Parent Action	Subsidiary Action	Parent Gain/Loss ($)	Subsidiary Gain/Loss ($)	Net ($)
1-02-76	200.40	Short	Lag	Payment			
1-05	201.40	Long	Payment	—	(250)		
3-31	191.70		—	—	(2,175)	2,175	(250)
4-01	191.70	Short	Lag	Payment			
6-30	179.40		Payment	—	3,075	3,075	6,150
7-01	179.40	Short	Lag	Payment			
7-28	180.60	Long	Payment	—	(300)		
9-30	169.10		—	—	(2,575)	2,575	300
10-01	169.10	Short	Lag	Payment			
11-18	173.20	Long	Payment	—	(1,025)		
12-30	176.30		—	—	875	(1,900)	(1,750)
1-03-77	170.10	Long	Payment	Lag			
3-31	178.40		—	Payment	2,075	2,075	4,150
4-01	178.40	Long	Payment	Lag			
6-30	179.50		—	Payment	275	275	550
7-01	179.50	Long	Payment	Lag			
9-30	184.40		—	Payment	1,225	1,225	2,450
10-30	184.40	Long	Payment	Lag			
12-30	200.20		—	Payment	3,950	3,950	9,900
1-03-78	200.20	Long	Payment	Lag			
3-31	194.60		—	Payment	(1,400)	(1,400)	(2,800)
4-03	194.60	Short	Lag	Payment			
6-21	193.70	Long	Payment	—	225		
6-30	194.10		—	—	(100)	125	250
7-03	194.10	Long	Payment	Lag			
9-29	206.50		—	Payment	3,100	3,100	6,200
10-02	206.50	Long	Payment	Lag			
11-16	205.70	Short	—	Payment		(200)	
12-29	215.70		—	—	2,300	(2,300)	(200)
1-02-79	204.90	Long	Payment	Lag			
2-01	197.90	Short	—	Payment		(1,750)	
3-30	208.40		—	—	875	(875)	(1,750)
4-02	208.40	Long	Payment	Lag			
6-29	218.60		—	Payment	2,550	2,550	5,100
7-02	218.60	Long	Payment	Lag			
9-14	221.00	Short	—	Payment		600	
9-28	223.20		—	—	1,150	(1,150)	600
10-01	223.20	Short	Lag	Payment			
11-19	222.20	Long	Payment	—	250		
12-31	224.60		—	—	350	(350)	250

197

TABLE 9.8. (Continued)

Date	Price	Model Direction	Parent Action	Subsidiary Action	Parent Gain/Loss ($)	Subsidiary Gain/Loss ($)	Net ($)
1-02-80	224.60	Long	Payment	Lag			
3-06	227.00	Short	—	Payment		600	
3-31	222.10		—	—	(625)	625	600
4-01	222.10	Short	Lag	Payment			
4-21	230.60	Long	Payment	—	(2,375)		
6-30	240.40		—	—	2,450	(4,825)	(4,750)
7-01	240.40	Long	Payment	Lag			
9-30	248.20		—	Payment	1,950	1,950	3,900
10-01	248.20	Long	Payment	Lag			
11-19	249.00	Short	—	Payment		200	
12-31	252.40		—	—	1,050	(1,050)	200
1-02-81	241.50	Long	Payment	Lag			
1-30	238.60	Short	—	Payment		(725)	
3-31	221.55		—	—	(4,987)	4,212	(5,622)
4-01	221.55	Short	Lag	Payment			
6-30	187.95		Payment	—	8,400	8,400	16,800
7-01	187.95	Short	Lag	Payment			
9-30	171.95		Payment	—	4,000	4,000	8,000
10-01	171.95	Short	Lag	Payment			
10-08	180.05	Long	Payment	—	(2,025)		
12-31	181.90		—	—	462	(2,488)	(4,051)
1-04-82	181.90	Long	Payment	Lag			
1-13	177.75	Short	—	Payment		(1,037)	
3-31	169.36		—	—	(3,137)	2,100	(2,104)
4-01	169.35	Short	Lag	Payment			
5-07	173.30	Long	Payment	—	(987)		
6-30	164.10		—	—	(1,312)	1,312	(987)
7-01	164.10	Short	Lag	Payment			
8-24	166.25	Long	Payment	—	(537)		
9-30	158.80		—	—	(1,325)	1,325	(537)
10-01	158.80	Short	Lag	Payment			
12-31	151.40		Payment	—	1,850	1,850	3,700
1-03-83	162.40	Short	Lag	Payment			
3-31	148.25		Payment	—	3,537	3,537	7,074
4-04	148.25	Short	Lag	Payment			
4-12	153.15	Long	Payment	—	(1,225)		
6-30	153.20		—	—	13	(1,238)	(2,403)
7-01	153.20	Short	Lag	Payment			
9-30	149.60		Payment	—	900	900	1,800
10-03	149.60	Short	Lag	Payment			
10-07	152.05	Long	Payment	—	(613)		
12-30	146.15		—	—	(863)	863	(613)

TABLE 9.8. (Continued)

Date	Price	Model Direction	Parent Action	Subsidiary Action	Parent Gain/Loss ($)	Subsidiary Gain/Loss ($)	Net ($)
1-03-84	146.15	Short	Lag	Payment			
2-15	144.44	Long	Payment	—	(428)		
3-30	144.30		—	—	(35)	463	(35)
4-02	114.30	Long	Payment	Lag			
4-05	144.62	Short	—	Payment		(420)	
6-29	153.30		—	—	(2,250)	1,830	(2,670)
7-02	135.30	Short	Lag	Payment			
9-28	121.90		Payment	—	3,350	3,350	6,700
10-01	121.90	Short	Lag	Payment			
11-07	125.90	Long	Payment	—	(1,000)		
12-29	113.34		—	—	(2,140)	2,140	(1,000)
1-02-85	113.34	Short	Lag	Payment			
3-19	111.93	Long	Payment	—	353		
3-29	122.08		—	—	2,185	(2,185)	353
4-01	122.08	Long	Payment	Lag			
6-28	129.73		—	Payment	1,913	1,913	3,825
7-01	129.73	Long	Payment	Lag			
9-06	132.78	Short	—	Payment		762	
9-30	139.53		—	—	2,450	(1,750)	1,462
10-01	139.53	Long	Payment	Lag			
12-31	146.03		—	Payment	1,625	1,625	3,250
Total							$62,042

Note: The data is Continua™ data. Gain/loss figures are basis one British pound futures contract.

Thus in this simple case the hedger netted approximately 14 percent return per year on lead/lag decisions based on modified hedge-and-hold timing. These results may be compared to covering each intercompany transaction with a standard hedge-and-hold forward/futures contract, where such actions would have produced a net loss (including commissions, etc.). Technical timing, even when applied to basic concepts like deciding when to pay one's bills, can be a powerful tool.

Commentary.   The analysis discussed was based on intercompany payables between a U.S. parent and its British subsidiary. All payables were invoiced in pounds. And although the results of the study suggest that there is money to be made in like situations, if the parent had instead invoiced all payables in U.S. dollars the currency risk would have been avoided altogether. This is done in many cases, but not all exchange risk management policies are so global. Note also that the study can be applied to intercompany transactions between subsidiaries or one-sided situations, such as payables to a foreign firm.

CROSS HEDGING LESS COMMON CURRENCIES

Hedging in any one of the five actively traded currencies may be accomplished in several ways. But what if the exposure is in another currency, one where there are no futures or options? If the transaction is too small or there are other problems it may not be possible to arrange a bank forward contract. There are still two or three practical possibilities. First, it may be possible to negotiate the transaction directly in the *home* currency. Or the transaction may be contracted in the foreign currency at a preset rate. In either case the currency risk is essentially hedged. But for the latter situation the negotiated exchange rate may be too high, especially if the foreign currency drops in value. Last, even though forwards, futures, and options are not available in the exposed currency, should it correlate well with one of the big five, a *surrogate* currency can be used for the hedge. New developments in the futures market may offer other possibilities as well. There are European Currency Unit (ECU) futures and U.S. Dollar Index futures. Both have the potential for hedging uses, but so far (1986) they are too new to have generated adequate data to research.

As an example we will take the case of Jack Z Confections, a Chicago candymaker who is purchasing a batch mixer from an Australian firm. The total price is $500,000 with a payment schedule of one-third at signing, one-third at delivery, and the last third on completion of the installation. The order must be placed by January 7, 1983 to avoid a price increase. Delivery is expected about five or six months from signing and installation is estimated to take two months. Jack Z found that the manufacturer expected payment in Australian dollars (A$). Discussions with his bank led him to conclude that a bank forward contract was not feasible because of the small amount and the indefinite term. Jack Z then checked the recent history of the Australian dollar. He found that a year ago one Australian dollar was worth $1.1240, six months back it stood at $1.0192, three months ago it was $0.9493, and on January 7 it was $0.9887. He concluded that the Australian currency had bottomed out in October and would soon be back to par or better. He feared that it might recover at the same rate it fell, so that by July it could be $1.0190, reaching $1.0685 by September. If he signed the contract on January 7 for $500,000 (U.S.), converted to Australian it would come to A$505,714. One-third (A$168,571) or US$166,666 would be paid at signing, so there is no risk for that part. But if the Australian dollar recovered as projected, the A$168,571 due in July would cost him US$171,774, and the final A$168,571 in September would cost US$180,118. The mixer initially priced at US$500,000 would end up costing US$518,558. With this possibility in mind Jack Z was pleased when the manufacturer agreed to make the contract at parity, or one U.S. dollar for one Australian dollar. The premium paid by Jack Z on the basis of the January 7 rate was US$5,714.

The equipment was delivered on time on July 1, 1983. By this time the Australian dollar had slipped to 0.8767 so that the initial payment (US$166,666) would have cost only US$146,116. When installation was complete on September 1 the Australian was at 0.8775 (US$146,294). In this case Jack Z Confections paid a premium for the forward with the vendor and lost on the other end as well. The net over payment was US$46,638 (US$5,714 premium + US$40.924 potential windfall from currency fluctuation). Of course, the market could have firmed as projected and the premium could have been well spent. The out-of-pocket expense to Jack Z Confections was US$505,714. But it could have been much less.

Let us now see if it would have been possible to use a surrogate currency for hedging the Australian dollar. We will do a one-year comparison with the big five currencies to see if there is adequate correlation for a surrogate hedge. In Table 9.9 we have posted weekly prices on the six currencies. Using the data in Table 9.9 we can calculate the correlation coefficients and the other pertinent

TABLE 9.9. WEEKLY CURRENCY PRICES

	Australian Dollar	British Pound	Canadian Dollar	Deutsche Mark	Swiss Franc	Japanese Yen
01-08-82	1.1240	1.9170	0.8431	0.4429	0.5479	0.4519
01-14	1.1540	1.8670	0.8376	0.4342	0.5394	0.4455
01-22	1.1120	1.8710	0.8370	0.4320	0.5389	0.4399
01-29	1.0960	1.8800	0.8358	0.4316	0.5417	0.4387
02-05	1.0925	1.8620	0.8295	0.4263	0.5311	0.4285
02-12	1.0887	1.8445	0.8256	0.4219	0.5266	0.4236
02-19	1.0815	1.8490	0.8218	0.4232	0.5308	0.4284
02-26	1.0737	1.8195	0.8139	0.4188	0.5263	0.4211
03-05	1.0704	1.8390	0.8256	0.4269	0.5411	0.4274
03-12	1.0592	1.7980	0.8228	0.4204	0.5326	0.4165
03-19	1.0565	1.8010	0.8187	0.4194	0.5270	0.4092
03-26	1.0532	1.7865	0.8139	0.4171	0.5226	0.4040
04-02	1.0515	1.7885	0.8156	0.4171	0.5150	0.0453
04-16	1.0482	1.7645	0.8205	0.4139	0.5081	0.4049
04-23	1.0544	1.7705	0.8172	0.4188	0.5080	0.4150
04-30	1.0615	1.8150	0.8205	0.4297	0.5118	0.4248
05-07	1.0685	1.8380	0.8183	0.4388	0.5316	0.4304
05-14	1.0618	1.8270	0.8082	0.4344	0.5139	0.4261
05-21	1.0582	1.8000	0.8095	0.4344	0.5098	0.4212
05-28	1.0508	1.7840	0.8041	0.4259	0.5008	0.4111
06-04	1.0485	1.7968	0.7997	0.4237	0.4933	0.4107
06-11	1.0405	1.7860	0.7933	0.4202	0.4926	0.4056
06-18	1.0243	1.7395	0.7743	0.4066	0.4721	0.3900
06-25	1.0210	1.7210	0.7758	0.4030	0.4699	0.3880
07-02	1.0192	1.7325	0.7776	0.4034	0.4742	0.3900
07-09	1.0161	1.7280	0.7852	0.4021	0.4730	0.3920
07-16	1.0131	1.7420	0.7933	0.4061	0.4807	0.3940
07-23	1.0050	1.7715	0.7962	0.4186	0.4958	0.4000
07-30	0.9920	1.7410	0.7968	0.4072	0.4780	0.3891
08-06	0.9853	1.7150	0.8009	0.4008	0.4701	0.3850
08-13	0.9757	1.7025	0.7987	0.3986	0.4664	0.3815
08-20	0.9754	1.7430	0.8099	0.4087	0.4838	0.3940
08-27	0.9735	1.7325	0.8067	0.4039	0.4751	0.3891
09-03	0.9681	1.7345	0.8078	0.4055	0.4798	0.3890
09-10	0.9618	1.7050	0.8078	0.3986	0.4662	0.3810
09-17	0.9587	1.7125	0.8108	0.3998	0.4695	0.3799
09-24	0.9548	1.7085	0.8115	0.3978	0.4619	0.3754
10-01	0.9493	1.6980	0.8094	0.3964	0.4608	0.3722
10-08	0.9480	1.7050	0.8110	0.3964	0.4660	0.3725
10-15	0.9464	1.7085	0.8140	0.3982	0.4673	0.3720

TABLE 9.9. (Continued)

	Australian Dollar	British Pound	Canadian Dollar	Deutsche Mark	Swiss Franc	Japanese Yen
10-22	0.9303	1.6965	0.8155	0.3947	0.4591	0.3650
10-29	0.9364	1.6780	0.8157	0.3909	0.4537	0.3640
11-05	0.9447	1.6640	0.8184	0.3879	0.4507	0.3630
11-12	0.9402	1.6560	0.8182	0.3868	0.4509	0.3731
11-19	0.9460	1.6210	0.8189	0.3937	0.4581	0.3891
11-26	0.9540	1.5960	0.8078	0.3986	0.4655	0.3995
12-03	0.9625	1.6435	0.8089	0.4122	0.4824	0.4057
12-10	0.9640	1.6120	0.8100	0.4074	0.4808	0.4098
12-17	0.9668	1.6100	0.8086	0.4144	0.4897	0.4109
12-22	0.9726	1.6075	0.8082	0.4160	0.4955	0.4162
12-31	0.9812	1.6200	0.8098	0.4199	0.4988	0.4271
01-07-83	0.9887	1.6085	0.8158	0.4283	0.5171	0.4364
07-01	0.8767	1.5340	0.8132	0.3937	0.4755	0.4180
09-01	0.8775	1.4985	0.8111	0.3711	0.4571	0.4050

Source: The Wall Street Journal.

statistics for each potential surrogate. In this short study we ignore any possible autocorrelation effects.

The correlations between all the currencies and the Australian dollar are high. They are:

	Australian/ British	Australian/ Canadian	Australian/ German	Australian/ Swiss	Australian/ Japanese
Correlation Coefficients	0.984	0.938	0.977	0.985	0.975
Correlation (R^2)	0.968	0.879	0.954	0.970	0.950
Standard Deviation of Correlation Coefficients	0.025	0.049	0.030	0.024	0.031
Standard Deviation Line	0.046	0.039	0.013	0.013	0.014

The best correlation with the Australian dollar lies either with the British pound or the Swiss franc. They are about equal in correlation, both being over .97. Likewise, the standard deviation of the correlation coefficient is nearly the same. Only in the deviation about a line described by the data does the Swiss franc fare better.

TABLE 9.10.   OPTIMIZED KELTNER MODEL RECOMMENDATIONS
FOR THE PERIOD JANUARY 1, 1983 THROUGH SEPTEMBER 30, 1983

Date	Export Price	Model Direction	Hedge Action	Risk Stop	Trade Gain/Loss (+ Commission)	Market Move	Hedge Net
1983							
1-03	162.40	Short	No entry				
3-31	148.25		Completed			3,537	3,537
4-04	148.25	Short	No entry				
4-12	153.15	Long	Entry	149.15			
6-14	152.89	Short	No exit	149.15			
6-24	155.20	Long	Continued	151.20			
6-27	153.37	Short	Continued				
6-30	153.20		Trade out		(112)		
6-30	153.20		Completed			(1,238)	(1,350)
7-01	153.20	Short	No entry				
9-30	149.60		Completed			900	900

Note: Gain/loss figures are for one contract of BP 25,000 and quoted in U.S. dollars.

For this study we will opt for the British pound because of our earlier work in this chapter.

Jack Z Confections will be hurt by an increase in value of the Australian dollar relative to the U.S. dollar. Thus for the period January through August 1983, Jack Z Confections must be long to be hedged. Starting on January 7, 1983, when the British pound is valued at 1.6085, the US$166,666 payment translates to BP 103,615 or four futures contracts on the IMM exchange (each contract is for BP 25,000). From January through June eight contracts are required for essentially full coverage; thereafter, only four. We will follow the long hedger example from earlier in the chapter, using the Continua data prices, which are only a linear step from the actual trading prices. The Keltner model recommendations from Table 9.1 are reproduced in Table 9.10 for ready reference.

No hedge is placed until April 12, 1983. This is held until June 30 for a loss of US$112 per contract or US$896 total (assuming a $100 commission per contract). No hedge was placed in the July through September quarter. The net to Jack Z Confections would be a US$40,028 windfall profit on the value loss of the Australian dollar. Had Jack Z followed the surrogate hedge path the net cost of the equipment would have been only US$460,000.

On the face of it, there was nothing particularly wrong with the analysis Jack Z Confections used that led them to the hedge-and-hold forward contract that they ended up with. No one could have guaranteed that the Australian dollar would take the dip it did. The rule, however, is to remain prepared for whatever eventuality the market presents. While not always more profitable than guessing, this approach offers the people like Jack Z Confections an alternative, one that is soundly based and does have a good probability of hedging the exposure properly.

NOTE

1. "CISCO Concensus Moving Average Index." *CISCO Review* 7, no. 5 (May 1983).

10
Organizing a Technical Hedge Group

The businessperson has enough problems with competition, pricing, market changes, and the like. Why then ask for new problems by getting into an alien field like currency hedging? The same question occurred to a number of manufacturers some years back on freight rates. The answer then was that there was money to be made figuring one's own rates instead of relying on the railroads. Similarly, today the answer for some trading companies is simply that there is a substantial amount of money to be made in the hedging function. A net loss area can be turned into a nonloser or even a profit center. Since exchange rate fluctuations are a disagreeable fact of life anyway, why not turn them to advantage?

The first step in organizing a group that is so far from the mainstream of most companies' effort is to obtain a commitment from management, preferably at the board of directors level. This follows naturally from the potential effect that such a group can have on the entire organization. The natural location is in the treasurer's office where, presumably, decisions are already being made on currency hedging. The high level approval and oversight are necessary because of the unfortunate fact that hedgers often tend to become speculators. The discipline that must be instilled can only come from above.

The group will need to detail its functions. These will vary from company to company, but we will list a sample set here.

1. Keep in touch with the foreign exchange markets. This deceptively easy job is a most important function. The best guess for the future behavior of a market is that it will continue what it is doing. This is called *momentum* and was discussed in Chapter 8.

2. Aid management in developing hedging policy. Many companies do their hedging by relying on outside sources such as banks. Often, more flexibility is needed and it can come only from within.

3. Stay current in legal, accounting, and tax requirements. All these areas tend to change regularly. It is possible for a good hedge at one time to be a poor one at another. The ability to keep up is a valuable function.

4. Act as liaison between top management and the hedging department. Often the departments view the information requirements for hedging as an unnecessary bother. A group with high level approval may be able to get the information.

5. Develop guidelines for exposure identification in the various departments. The lack of definitive information for hedging (in time) often derives from the department not knowing far enough ahead of time that certain data would be needed. Set up guidelines for identifying and detailing exposures to the department.

6. Evaluate the technical bases for hedging decisions. Hedging models, economic services, data sources, and the like vary in quality, cost, and applicability. Only by being up-to-date is it possible to make rational choices.

7. Maintain liaison with those providing the company with hedging services. The group can provide the focus and the filter for the outside services. The better prepared the group is, the better the deal on the hedge. Commissions can be negotiated, terms may be adjusted, and so forth.

8. Develop in-house research capacity. If a firm is large enough, it may make economic sense to build a research group within the hedge group. The principal danger is a *not invented here* syndrome that could lead to the exclusion of worthwhile outside services.

9. *Face a sunset review annually.* If the group is providing worthwhile economic functions there will be no trouble in justifying its continued existence. Otherwise, it should be terminated. Additional self-perpetuating bureaucracy is hardly needed.

These are certainly not all the functions a hedging group might perform. Some groups might only do one or two; some groups might consist of only one or two people. But, properly handled a hedging group can perform a valuable function.

Appendix 1
FAS-52 Summary

Introduced in January 1978, FAS-8, "Accounting For the Translation of Foreign Currency Transactions and Foreign Currency Financial Statements" met considerable opposition throughout the business community. In response, the Financial Accounting Standards Board (FASB) revised FAS-8 and presented FAS-52, "Foreign Currency Translation" in December 1981.[1]

This summary is intended to provide a general understanding of the workings of FAS-52 and how it can influence foreign currency transactions and the translation of foreign currency financial statements. The summary begins by first introducing the ruling's major deviation from FAS-8, the *functional currency* concept. We then proceed through FAS-52 in an attempt to highlight its key points. It must be stressed that the following is only a summary. Consult your tax and accounting professionals for direct applications.

THE FUNCTIONAL CURRENCY

The functional currency is the currency used in the economic environment in which a particular firm operates (the environment in which it primarily generates and expends cash). The functional currency dictates whether the firm uses only *current* exchange rates or a combination of current and *historical* exchange rates in translating its foreign statements. Guidelines for the determination of the functional currency are provided by FAS-52. However, management's judgment is also important in the decision. The following factors help to determine the functional currency:

1. Cash flow indicators
2. Sales price indicators
3. Sales market indicators
4. Expense indicators
5. Intercompany transactions and arrangements indicators

Once the functional currency is established, the books of record are to be maintained in that currency. If the books are not kept in the functional currency they must be remeasured into the functional currency prior to translation into the reporting currency. Since the books must appear as if they initially had been recorded in the functional currency, some accounts are to be remeasured using historical exchange rates while others are to be remeasured using current rates. Appendix B of FAS-52 outlines these accounts and the rates to be used.

ACCOUNTING FOR FOREIGN CURRENCY TRANSLATION

A. If the U.S. dollar is the functional currency (the foreign operation is an extension of the parent's domestic operations):
  1. Exchange rate fluctuations relate to individual assets and liabilities and impact the parent's cash flows directly.
  2. Translation adjustments (exchange gains and losses) are recognized currently in net income as a nonoperating item.
B. If a foreign currency is the functional currency (the foreign operation is relatively self-contained and integrated within the foreign country):

1. Exchange rate fluctuations relate to the net investment in that operation and not individual assets and liabilities.
2. Translation adjustments due to consolidating that foreign operation do not impact cash flows and are not included in determing net income.
3. Translation adjustments are accumulated and disclosed in a separate component of equity.
4. On the sale or nearly complete liquidation of the net investment in the foreign entity, the amount attributable to that entity and accumulated in the translation adjustment component of equity is removed and reported as a part of the gain or loss on the sale or liquidation of the asset.

C. Conditions determining current and/or historical exchange rates:
   1. When the U.S. dollar is the functional currency:
      a. Both current and historical rates are used, depending on the type of account being translated.
      b. In the case of many transactions, as in revenue and expense accounts, appropriately weighted averages of exchange rates may be used for simplification.
   2. When a foreign currency is the functional currency:
      a. The current exchange rate is used for all balance sheet accounts.
      b. Weighted averages as in C1b above are also allowed.
   3. Table A1.1 outlines the applicable rates, current or historic, for each balance sheet account.

ACCOUNTING FOR FOREIGN CURRENCY TRANSACTIONS

A change in exchange rates (between the functional currency and the foreign currency to be received or paid) that increases or decreases the expected cash flow amount on settlement of the transaction is known as a transaction gain or loss.

A. The transaction gain or loss is usually included in determining net income for the period in which the exchange rate changes.

TABLE A1.1. RATES USED TO TRANSLATE ASSETS AND LIABILITIES

	U.S. Dollar Is Functional Currency		Foreign Currency Is Functional Currency	
	Current	Historical	Current	Historical
Assets				
Cash, deman and time deposits	X		X	
Marketable equity securities:				
Carried at cost		X	X	
Carried at current market price	X		X	
Accounts and notes receivable	X		X	
Allowance for doubtful accounts and notes receivable	X		X	
Inventories:				
Carried at cost		X	X	
Carried at current replacement or selling price	X		X	
Carried at net realizable value	X		X	
Carried at contract price	X		X	
Prepaid insurance, advertising, and rent		X	X	
Refundable deposits	X		X	
Advances to unconsolidated subsidiaries	X		X	
Property, plant, and equipment		X	X	
Accumulated depreciation of property, plant, and equipment		X	X	
Cash surrender value of life insurance	X		X	
Patents, trademarks, licenses, and formulas		X	X	
Goodwill		X	X	
Other tangible assets		X	X	
Liabilities				
Accounts and notes payable and overdrafts	X		X	
Accrued expense payable	X		X	
Accrued losses on firm purchase commitments	X		X	
Refundable deposits	X		X	
Deferred income		X	X	
Bonds payable or other long-term debt	X		X	
Unamortized premium of discount on bonds or notes payable	X		X	
Convertible bonds payable	X		X	
Accrued pension obligations	X		X	
Obligations and warranties	X		X	

Note: Reprinted from FAS-52, Appendix A.

B. The accounting method for all transactions except forward contracts is as follows:

   1. Each transaction is measured and recorded in the functional currency using the current exchange rate in effect when the transaction is recorded.
   2. On the balance sheet date, balances denominated in a currency other than the functional currency should be adjusted to reflect the current exchange rate

C. Forward exchange contracts:

KEY

SR_b = Spot rate at balance sheet date
SR_o = Spot rate at inception of forward contract
FR_c = Contracted forward rate
FR_r = Forward rate available on the remaining
       maturity of the contract

   1. Gains or losses (except for those discussed in D) are included in determining net income in the same manner as other foreign currency transactions. Agreements that are essentially the same as forwards, that is, currency swaps, futures, and so forth, are accounted for in the same manner as forward contracts.
   2. Calculation of forward contract gain or loss (whether or not deferred):

$$\text{G/L} = \text{Amount of contract} * (SR_b\text{-}SR_o)$$

   The formula does not apply to speculative forward contracts (see 4 following).
   3. Calculation of discount or premium on a forward contract:

$$\text{Disc/Prem} = \text{Amount of contract} * (FR_c\text{-}SR_o)$$

   The forward discount or premium is accounted for separately from the gain or loss (G/L) on the contract, and is amortized (expensed) over the life of the contract (straight-line method).
   4. Speculative forward contracts (those that do not hedge a foreign currency exposure):

a. G/L = Amount of contract $*$ (FR_r-FR_c)

b. The discount or premium is not recognized separately

c. Gains and losses are recognized currently

D. The following types of transaction gains and losses are excluded from the determination of net income:

1. Economic hedges of a net investment in a foreign entity. Gains and losses on these transactions are reported in the same manner as in B.

2. Intercompany foreign currency transactions that are of a long-term-investment nature (i.e., settlement is not planned or anticipated in the forseeable future), when the entities to the transaction are consolidated, combined, or accounted for by the equity method in the reporting entity's financial statements. Gains and losses on such transactions are reported in the same manner as in B.

3. A forward contract or other foreign currency commitment intended to hedge an identifiable foreign currency commitment.

   a. Gains and losses are deferred and included in the measurement of the related foreign currency transaction.

   b. Losses should not be deferred if their deferral will lead to recognizing losses in later periods.

   c. A foreign currency transaction is considered a hedge of an identifiable foreign currency commitment if:

      i. The foreign currency commitment is designated and effective as a hedge of a foreign currency commitment.

      ii. The foreign currency commitment is firm.

   d. The portion of the hedging accounted for is limited to the amount of the related commitment.

      i. That portion exceeding the amount of the related commitment but is intended as a hedge on an after-tax basis is deferred.

      ii. Any portion exceeding the amount on an after-tax basis is not deferrable.

TAXATION

A. Interperiod tax allocation is required for those taxable or tax deductable exchange gains or losses that are included in net income in one period for financial statement purposes and in a different period for tax purposes.

B. Translation adjustments are generally accounted for like timing differences under APB Opinions 11, 12, and 24. There are exceptions for deferred taxes for unremitted earnings of a subsidiary (FAS-52 para. 23).

C. Income tax expense is to be allocated among income before extraordinary items, adjustments of prior periods, and direct entries to other equity accounts. Income taxes related to translation gains and losses and translation adjustments should be allocated to that separate component of equity.

THE APPROPRIATE EXCHANGE RATES TO BE USED, AND WHEN

A. For foreign currency transactions:
   1. Use the applicable exchange rate on settlement of the transaction.
   2. On the balance sheet date the current exchange rate should be used.

B. For foreign currency statements the exchange rate used to convert dividends of a currency for purposes of dividend remittances should be used.

NOTE

1. Summary drawn from SFAS No. 52 "Foreign Currency Translation" Financial Accounting Standards Board, December 1981.

Appendix 2
FAS-52 and Foreign Currency Options

A summary of the accounting rules as they pertain to foreign currency options is presented here. The summary is drawn from "PHLX, Foreign Currency Options, Tax and Accounting Considerations," a study prepared by Arthur Andersen & Co. and the Philadelphia Stock Exchange. This summary is not intended to provide specific legal, accounting, or other professional advice, but rather to provide a practical overview of the accounting implications of foreign currency options. Options are considered for hedging purposes only; their use for speculative purposes is not addressed.

FORWARDS VS. OPTIONS

The accounting for foreign currency options closely follows the forward contract principles outlined in FAS-52 (summarized in Appendix 1). However, there are some basic differences that should be noted.

SR_b = Spot rate at balance sheet date
SR_o = Spot rate at inception of forward contract
FR_c = Contracted forward rate

219

FR_r = Forward rate available on the remaining
maturity of the contract

A. Gain/loss (G/L) calculations
   1. Forward contracts: Accounting G/L = Amount of contract $*$ (SR_b-SR_o)
   2. Option contracts: The gain or loss on an option is dependent on the current market value of the option; any *real* loss is limited to the total option premium paid.
B. Discount/Premium
   1. Forward contracts: Disc/Prem = Amount of contract $*$ (FR_c-SR_o)
   2. Option contracts: The option premium is the amount the option buyer/seller pays/receives when either purchasing or writing the option. (The buyer of an option pays a premium for that option.)

THE ACCOUNTING FOR HEDGING TRANSACTIONS

A. Transactions that are excluded from net income: Specific forward foreign exchange transactions qualify as a hedge and are consequently not included in the determination of net income (these are outlined in Appendix 1). They are listed in the following list as they would apply to options.
   1. The purchase of an option to hedge a foreign currency commitment.
      a. Accounting for transactions of this sort is dependent on the two conditions previously stated in Appendix 1, Accounting for Foreign Currency Transactions, D, 3c.
      b. The option premium is considered a cost of limiting risk on the commitment being hedged, and is deferred until the commitment is settled. The premium is included in the measurement of the revenue or expense associated with the commitment.
      c. If the commitment is canceled before the option is exer-

cised, gains or losses deferred prior to cancellation should be charged or credited against net income.

2. The purchase of an option to hedge a net investment in a foreign entity. The accounting for gains or losses resulting from the option should parallel the accounting for translation adjustments (Appendix 1, Accounting for Foreign Currency Transactions, B).

B. Transactions that are included in net income

1. The purchase of an option to hedge a net asset or liability position. As with forwards, gains and losses resulting from a hedge of this nature should be reflected in current net income.

2. The purchase of an option that is not intended for hedging purposes (as described previously). Transactions of this nature are generally considered speculative; gains or losses are included in current net income.

3. The sale of an option. Writing options is generally viewed as speculative. Gains or losses on such transactions are included in current net income.

Appendix 3
Currency Options on the PHLX and IMM: Specifications

CURRENCY OPTIONS ON THE PHLX

Currency	Contract Size	Quotation Units	Strike Price Intervals (In cents)	Minimum Contract Price Change
British pound	BP 12,500	Cents/BP	5	.05 = $6.25
Deutsche mark	DM 62,500	Cents/DM	2	.01 = $6.25
Japanese yen	JY 6,250,000	Cents/JY	.01	.01 = $6.25
Swiss franc	SF 62,500	Cents/SF	2	.01 = $6.25
Canadian dollar	CD 50,000	Cents/CD	1	.01 = $5.00

Settlement: Cash settled.
Last day of trading: 1:30 P.M. (EST) on the first business day before expiration.

Source: Understanding Foreign Currency Options, The Third Dimension to Foreign Exchange, the Philadelphia Stock Exchange.

CURRENCY OPTIONS ON THE IMM

Currency	Contract Size	Quotation Units	Strike Price Intervals (In cents)	Minimum Contract Price Change
British pound	BP 25,000	Cents/BP	2.5	.5 = $12.50
Deutsche mark	DM 125,000	Cents/DM	1	.01 = $12.50
Japanese yen	JY 12,500,000	Cents/JY	.01	.01 = $12.50
Swiss franc	SF 125,500	Cents/SF	1	.01 = $12.50
Canadian dollar	CD 100,000	Cents/CD	1	.01 = $10.00

Settlement: Results in a futures position.

Last day of trading: Two Fridays before the third Wednesday of contract month.

Source: Trading and Hedging with Currency Options, the Chicago Mercantile Exchange, 1985.

Appendix 4

Currency Futures (Traded on the IMM): Specifications

Currency	Contract Size	Quotation Units	Minimum Contract Price Change	
British pound	BP 25,000	$/BP	.0005	= $12.50
Deutsche mark	DM 125,000	$/DM	.0001	= $12.50
Japanese yen	JY 12,500,000	$/JY	(.00)0001	= $12.50
Swiss franc	SF 125,000	$/SF	.0001	= $12.50
Canadian dollar	CD 100,000	$/CD	.0001	= $10.00
French franc	FR 250,000	$/FR	.00005	= $12.50
Mexican peso	MP 1,000,000	$/MP	.00001	= $10.00

Contract months traded: March, June, September, and December
Last day of trading: Two business days before the third Wednesday of the delivery month.

Source: Trading and Hedging With Currency Options, the Chicago Mercantile Exchange, 1985.

Appendix 5
Forwards, Futures, and Options: A Comparison between Instruments

The following table briefly compares forwards, futures, exchange traded options, and bank negotiated options over a variety of categories. More detailed comparisons can be found in their respective chapters.

	Forward	Future	Exchange Option	Bank Option
Currency selection	Wide	BP, CD, JY, SF, DM.[a]	BP, CD, JY, SF, DM[a].	Major world currencies
Contract exchange rate	Calculated forward rate, market driven	Market driven	Varying exercise rates	Varying exercise rates
Type of market	Interbank market	Auction market	Auction market	Issuing bank only
Delivery dates	Negotiated for any date	Limited to four times per year	Limited to four times per year	Negotiated for any date
Early liquidation capability	Unavailable or involves stiff penalty	Available anytime at prevailing rate	Anytime prior to expiration	Anytime prior to expiration
Costs	Premium/Discount paid on settlement date, net expense is unknown until settlement date	Upfront cost is equal to opportunity cost of margin req. (90% can earn T-bill rate), net expense	Maximum cost is known upfront	Maximum cost is known upfront

	Forward	Future	Exchange Option	Bank Option
		is unknown until settlement		
Commissions	Implicit in bid/ask spread	Negotiable	Negotiable	Within premium paid
Contract size	Any size (Usually greater than $500,000)	Standardized size, approximately $50,000 or any multiple	Standardized size, approximately $25,000 or any multiple	Any size (Usually greater than $500,000)
Performance guarantee	Dependent on financial integrity of opposing party	Guaranteed by clearing house	Guaranteed by clearing house	Dependent on financial integrity of issuing bank

[a]BP is British pound, CD is Canadian dollar, JY is Japanese yen, SF is Swiss franc, and DM is deutsche mark. Actively traded currencies on U.S. exchanges. Other currencies are offered but see little actual trading.

Appendix 6
Table of Volatility: 1976–1985

Year	Quarter	Deutsche Mark	Japanese Yen	Canadian Dollar	Swiss Franc	British Pound
1976	1	5.6	1.8	3.7	4.2	6.5
	2	3.5	1.5	1.3	5.7	9.4
	3	6.0	4.1	2.2	3.8	8.3
	4	4.0	4.1	6.1	2.0	10.7
1977	1	3.8	6.3	5.1	6.3	4.7
	2	2.4	4.4	1.6	3.3	1.7
	3	4.4	2.7	2.0	5.1	3.3
	4	10.0	9.7	3.0	16.4	8.4
1978	1	7.1	10.6	4.2	12.0	5.0
	2	7.4	12.7	4.4	9.9	4.7
	3	7.5	11.3	5.7	25.1	6.4
	4	13.9	15.5	3.4	21.5	6.7
1979	1	5.8	12.4	3.6	9.2	5.5
	2	4.9	7.1	2.0	6.7	7.1
	3	6.7	7.2	2.3	7.8	8.4
	4	5.8	15.2	3.3	11.1	8.7
1980	1	16.7	11.9	5.1	21.5	6.1
	2	11.0	20.5	3.3	14.9	9.4
	3	5.3	10.4	2.3	7.9	5.3
	4	13.5	9.0	4.8	16.0	4.4
1981	1	17.4	11.1	2.2	19.9	11.3
	2	15.5	9.6	2.4	14.9	16.8
	3	15.2	10.6	4.8	15.4	11.2
	4	7.3	10.5	3.5	12.4	9.3

Year	Quarter	Deutsche Mark	Japanese Yen	Canadian Dollar	Swiss Franc	British Pound
1982	1	9.9	17.8	4.1	11.6	9.0
	2	11.2	14.2	6.9	16.8	7.6
	3	5.7	12.0	6.3	12.1	5.4
	4	11.5	23.0	2.6	14.7	9.7
1983	1	7.3	7.4	1.7	10.6	11.8
	2	7.8	5.8	1.6	6.1	8.4
	3	8.8	5.0	1.0	6.1	4.7
	4	9.2	3.4	1.9	8.0	7.5
1984	1	10.8	5.0	2.7	6.8	6.9
	2	7.9	13.9	3.3	8.5	6.3
	3	11.3	2.7	2.9	8.8	7.8
	4	7.6	3.6	1.5	7.8	9.3
1985	1	10.9	4.9	5.7	12.3	16.7
	2	10.3	5.0	4.4	11.4	10.2
	3	12.7	17.8	2.3	15.6	10.7
	4	10.3	8.2	2.6	7.0	5.6

Note: Volatility expressed as percentage of the average exchange rate over the corresponding quarter.

Appendix 7
Foreign Exchange Hedging Survey:[1] Survey Questionnaire and Results

1. Does your firm engage in any foreign currency denominated transactions or hold oversease assets?

    [37] yes   66%
    [19] no . . . if no, please skip to question 15. 34%

2. In these transactions, what are the most common currencies you deal in?

    [28] British pound   76%   [21] Japanese yen   58%
    [6] Swiss franc   16%   [22] Canadian dollar   59%
    [20] Deutche mark   54%   [12] French franc   32%
    [ ] other; could you please name a few:

       a. Australian dollar 14%   d. Mexican peso   8%
       b. Dutch guilder   11%   e. Belgian franc   8%
       c. Italian lire   11%

Others:
            Brazilian cruzeiro   Saudi rial
            South African rand   Chinese renminbi

Spanish peseta   Irish pound

Singapore dollar   Hong Kong dollar

Danish krone   Malaysian ringgit

3. What is your average foreign exchange transaction and/or exposure size (approximate)? * anonymity will be preserved.

[16] less than $1 million (US$ terms)   43%

[21] greater than $1 million   57%

4. Has a foreign exchange hedging policy been defined by your board of directors?

		large	small
[7] yes	19%	29%	6%
[30] no	81%	71%	94%

5. Do you hedge your foreign currency transactions and/or exposures?

		large	small
[28] yes	76%	90%	56%
[9] no	24%	10%	44%

If no, not hedging is a result of:

[2] company policy

[3] the costs outweigh the benefits

[6] our exposures tend to balance each other out

[2] other

If you answer to question 5 is "no," please skip questions 6–12.

6. How has your hedging/risk management activity reacted to the changes in accounting for foreign exchange translation caused by the revision of FAS-8 to FAS-52?

[9] less activity   32%

[16] no change   57%

[1] greater activity   4%

[2] no answer

7. Which of the following hedging methods do you use?

[26] forward foreign exchange contracts   93%

[3] futures contracts   11%

[2] bank foreign exchange options   7%

[1] exchange-traded foreign exchange options

[20] internal corporate techniques, e.g.,   71%
     asset/liability management, pricing policies,
     leading and lagging of payables and receivables,
     etc.

[1] technically oriented hedging methods

8. In your experience with the forward exchange and futures markets, how would you rate these markets based on their ability to properly hedge your exposures?

The forward market:

[17] good 65%   [9] fair 35%   [0] poor

The futures market:

[3] good 30%   [7] fair 70%   [0] poor

9. In general, how would you describe your foreign exchange hedging objectives?

		large	small
[9] minimize losses	32%	32%	33%
[7] come out even	25%	16%	44%
[12] minimize losses, but also take advantage potential exchange gains.	43%	53%	22%

10. How often do you evaluate your foreign exchange forecasts?

		large	small
[5] daily	19%	22%	—
[3] weekly	12%	14%	13%
[14] monthly	54%	36%	63%
[4] quarterly	15%	14%	25%
[0] semiannually			
[2] never	8%		
[1] as needed			
[1] no answer			

11. Do you use any methods to determine hedge placement timing?

		large	small
[11] yes 39%		47%	11%
[17] no 61%		47%	89%

If yes, is this analysis done

[10] in-house?	100%	—
[5] by an outside service?	44%	—

12. Who manages your foreign exchange hedging?

[28] yourself	100%
[0] your bank(s)	
[0] an outside service	

13. Who do you consult for your foreign exchange information?

[10] your own in-house group	27%
[11] your subsidiaries	30%

[35] your bank(s)   97%

[11] some other outside service   30%

14. Are you aware of any educational foreign exchange hedging programs currently offered?

[14] yes   38%

[21] no   56%

[2] no answer

If yes, where?

For those not currently involved in Foreign Currency Transactions:

15. Does your company anticipate having foreign currency denominated transactions in the near future (1–2 years)?

[4] yes

[15] no

16. If so, have you given foreign exchange hedging any formal consideration up to this point?

[1] yes

[8] no

17. Are you aware of any educational foreign exchange hedging programs currently offered?

[2] yes

[17] no

If yes, where?

NOTE

1. Survey conducted by CISCO, Commodity Information Services Co., Chicago, IL, 1984.

Index